THE
PREPPER'S
Pantry

Building and Thriving with Food Storage

ANNE LANG

The Prepper's Pantry
Building and Thriving on Food Storage
Anne Lang

Copyright © 2012 (Anne Lang)

The information contained in this book is true and complete to the best of our knowledge. All recommendations are made without guarantee on the part of the author or publisher. Note: Many of the procedures described in this book are subject to the US Department of Agriculture guidelines. Readers are cautioned to refer to the most current USDA guidelines for the most current recommendations.

Visit our website at www.preppers-pantry.com.

ISBN-10:0-9854783-0-6
ISBN-13: 978-0-9854783-0-8

Printed in the United States of America

Cover design by Karrie Ross
Cover photos by iStockphoto.com

First Edition: April, 2012

DEDICATION

Dedicated to my husband, Larry, who loves and supports me in all I do, and to my mother, Suzanne, who always told me I could do anything.

Contents

1

Food Storage

There is something innate in human nature that calls us to put up food. An inner whisper, borne from thousands of years of dependence on seasonal food. Our very survival was once dependent on our ability to store food. This day may come again.

So you've decided to prepare for potential disaster by storing food and water for your family. Good thinking. There are many potential hazards, from job loss to power outages, to more drastic doomsday scenarios. Hopefully, none of these things will happen to you, but if they do, some advance planning can make a dramatic difference in the quality of life for you and your family.

I won't go into all of the possible scenarios for which we could possibly need to prepare; there are endless sources of speculation on all forms of media. My focus is on providing food for my family in case it is needed, in times of hardship. This may also include the lack of electricity, or other typical fuels for cooking.

This book will help you learn what and how much food to store, options for storing the food including over 200 recipes for nourishing, delicious meals straight from your food storage.

Whether or not a world-changing event occurs, having sufficient food stores planned for your family brings peace of mind, and is an excellent hedge against inflation. In building your food storage, you can leverage volume pricing, and in rotating and using this stock, your average cost of food will decrease.

Don't be intimidated by the amount of food needed to store. Start with a week, build to a month, and then increase until you've met your goal. Remember the adage "How do you eat an elephant? One bite at a time." Divide up the tasks and purchases for building your food storage into steps which will work for you.

2

Setting Your Goal

The first step in building your food storage is to determine the ultimate goal. First decide the scenarios for which you will prepare; a short-term emergency where services will likely be restored in a matter of days, or a potentially long-term scenario where your family will need to provide its own food for months or possibly indefinitely.

In the worst case scenario, where we would need to secure food for a family indefinitely, you'll need to figure out how long it would take your family to establish a garden and grow all your own food on an ongoing basis and plan for enough food to sustain you until your garden can be established.

A very common approach is to store food for a year or more. If, for example, it would be possible to grow a garden to produce your vegetables, it might be a good choice to store fruits and vegetables for a year, and your rice, wheat and beans for a longer period of time.

Once you have established the length of time for which you'd like to prepare, determine how many people you want to include in your planning. Consider also, if you can increase the total to be able to share with those in need.

Don't be alarmed if your goal seems daunting. The point is to identify your goal, and then to begin working toward it

3

Planning Abundance

Food has differing shelf lives. I organize my food storage based on its shelf life. I also plan meals I know my family will enjoy and I plan to have plenty of food available. I want to feed my family abundantly, with variety and have enough to share as I can.

If you plan to survive well for a year, hopefully that means you can sustain your family indefinitely going forward, with some wise advance planning and some hard work. And if we don't wind up needing our food storage, that's okay too. Once you've got your food storage, it is a win-win situation.

The Deep Larder

The deep larder is where I store foods which will last 10 – 30 years. Most grain, dehydrated food and milk can be stored for very long times when properly packaged and stored. Items in the deep larder include wheat, corn, rice, beans, oats, pasta, sugar and dehydrated fruits and vegetables.

Be sure to choose a cool, dark, dry location for your deep larder to maximize the shelf life of your food. Ideally the area will be away from insects, rodents and other pests. Some families choose to bury or hide their deep larder. It might be advisable to split your deep larder up into several locations. Plan to inventory your deep larder once a year and move any items which will be expiring within a year up to your rotation pantry.

4

How Much To Store

One Year Supply	Column A Men, active teens or very active women.	Column B Most women, children over 6 and seniors.	Column C Children under 6
Wheat (and pasta)	275 lbs.	175 lbs.	60 lbs.
Other Grains	125 lbs.	115 lbs.	50 lbs.
Legumes (Beans, Peas, Lentils)	75 lbs.	50 lbs.	15 lbs.
Corn	60 lbs.	50 lbs.	40 lbs
Sweeteners (Sugar, Honey, Jam)	65 lbs.	60 lbs.	40 lbs.
Powdered Milk*	60 lbs.	60 lbs.	80 lbs.
Eggs-#10 cans*	2 cans	2 cans	1 cans
Salt	10 lbs. per person per year		
Oil/Fat	2.5 gallons	2.5 gallons	2.5 gallons

One Year Supply	Column A Men, active teens or very active women.	Column B Most women, children over 6 and seniors.	Column C Children under 6
Water	3 gallons per day	3 gallons per day	3 gallons per day
Fruit / Veg-tables	To preference. I allow 2 cups per person per day. Store at minimum apples, onions, celery, carrots and potatoes (flakes, shreds, diced and sliced).		

To insure I have what my family enjoys, I select a year's worth of meals and calculate the ingredients and then I double-check my storage against the guidelines above. You can choose as few as a week's (or two) worth of breakfasts and dinners, and multiplying that by 52 (or 26) to calculate your food storage needs. I prefer a bit more detail selecting some items we'd eat weekly, such as various kinds of tacos, and other items we'd like to have once a month or so, and I adjusted our plan for seasonality as that big bowl of chili is far more appealing in December than it is in the heat of August.

I also plan for lunch and snacks for my family. We are big eaters, and if we were to revert to an agrarian society, there is much more work to be done and appetites will adjust accordingly. Visualize for a moment, the work in involved in doing a load of laundry without electricity or running water. Yes, pioneer people have big appetites and I don't want anyone going hungry. To that end I planned to serve a protein for at least two of the three meals daily, and I plan at least two cups of fruits and vegetables per person daily and plenty of fresh bread to accompany meals. No one will starve on my watch.

Important: Be sure to purchase a grain mill to grind your wheat and corn.

Plan to inventory your deep larder once a year and move anything which will expire in the coming year into your rotation pantry.

Important: Purchase several can openers if you are storing #10 cans and several bucket openers and Gamma lids if you are storing buckets.

Tips:

- Buy a grain mill to be able to grind wheat and corn for use.

- Buy lots of can openers, can lids, bucket openers and gamma lids to be able to open and reclose your food.

- Plan to have more water and salt than you think you will need.

- Plan to be able to share with those in need.

- Plan to have cards, games and other activities available to occupy your family.

- Store some cash or coin.

- Store extra items which could be given as charity or traded for items you need.

5

The Rotation Pantry

The rotation pantry is where I store all of the commercial canned goods we like to eat as well as all of the pressure canned meats which I keep in rotation and which I plan to eat within a year or two. I also keep bagged/canned dinners here and bread kits as well as flour, yeast, and other items with shorter shelf lives.

I keep a close eye on my rotation pantry, because I need to replace items as they are used to keep my goal of a 1 – 2 year supply. Also, I make a point to serve my bagged/canned dinners once or twice a week to keep these items rotated and fresh. I resupply these items quarterly and try to keep an abundant supply. These meals also make it easy to share a meal with friends in need.

A good approach to building your food storage over time is to begin by building your rotation pantry by buying extra canned goods every time you shop. It's also a good way to get started building your food storage, by storing bagged meals in your rotation pantry.

Be sure to locate your rotation pantry in an easily accessible location, but is preferably cool and dark.

Canned/Bagged Meals

My approach includes mylar bags with complete meal kits. Similar to a homemade MRE (Meals Ready to Eat), meal kits contain all the ingredients necessary to make a soup, stew or casserole; just add water. Some of my meals require a pint of pressure canned meat, and if so, I package those too.

Bread in a Bag

My approach also includes mylar bags filled with all the ingredients needed to make a loaf of bread, rolls or cornbread, or other bread in my rotation pantry. I plan to serve these to my family these about twice a week and replenish them
quarterly to keep my rotation pantry fresh as well as my skills at bread making.

Active Pantry

The active pantry is where I store cereal, crackers, snack foods and the items we eat every day. I don't inventory this pantry, I simply keep it stocked.

6

Your Prepper's Pantry

After you decide how many people and how long you will store, the next step to decide the incremental steps you will take to reach your goal. You can start with a month or three, or a whole year or ten depending on finances, space and other considerations. Alternately, you can plan to have your food storage in place by a certain timeframe and develop a plan to work towards that goal. Below are some example approaches.

Kim is a stay-at-home mom with 4 small children. Her husband, Bill provides for their family with his job in construction, but is subject to seasonal layoffs depending on the weather. Kim has a budget $200 per month to build her food stores. She spends half on long term storage items for her deep larder and half on canned goods for her rotation pantry. She buys $100 worth of grains or beans which she stores in #10 cans. She and a group of girlfriends bought a dry pack can sealer and share it. She spends her other $100 on buying double canned goods every time she shops at the grocery store. Kim calculates she can cook out of her pantry for 2 – 3 months now in case Bill is laid off. She is working towards having a whole year of food for her family.

Jane and her husband John both work in corporate jobs. They've recently gotten into prepping, and have agreed to spend $5 – 10K on food stores, but would like to have it in place before the end of the year. They plan to hide their deep larder by burying it in metal bins in several locations. John is building the storage locations and Jane is buying their food. She's calculated the number of pounds of food she'll purchase, and is buying her fruits and vegetables from an online retailer and storing beans and grains in 5 gallon buckets lined with mylar bags.

Julie is both a foodie and a planner. She's been through a couple of life events where her pantry served her well. She was without power for over a week after the Northridge earthquake and her home was recently affected by a widespread power outage that impacted several counties in her area and prompted her husband to give her the go-ahead to implement a full food storage pantry.

She calculated the amount of food to store based on the recommendations in this book. She bought about a third of it initially and plans to buy the rest over a few months, and to get more for her money, she is dehydrating, canning and packaging her own food. She believes she can make tastier food than she can buy commercially packaged and freeze-dried. She is adapting her recipes to work with dehydrated food and testing them on her family. When she gets a thumbs-up on a recipe, she adds it to the spreadsheet where she is tracking ingredients to make a year's worth of food. By the time she has her full year built up, she'll have fined-tuned her recipes and quantities so she'll have exactly what she needs to make the food her family likes best.

Debbie is a super-busy working mom, and has a be-prepared outlook on life. She has meal-in-a-bag kits lining the shelves in her pantry. Each kit has all the ingredients (even the water – in plastic bottles) to make a meal. She plans to make a year's supply of these and have them standing by to grab and go in case of an emergency where she needs to leave her home quickly. She finds the meals really handy to make on her busiest days. She can start a crock pot and pour in soup or stew ingredients, and be off to take her sons to baseball practice, and have dinner ready and waiting when they arrive home hours later.

To create your own approach to building your pantry you can use one or all of these ideas. If you plan to store meal kits, or plan specific recipes, be sure to taste test them with your family before you store mass quantities. That's a good idea for people buying powdered meal mixes – do taste test them to make sure they are palatable to your family.

To adapt recipes to cooking, refer to the chapter on converting recipes, and also the information about yields. Once you have a recipe successfully adapted and selected for your meal rotation, determine how often you'd like to have it, and "annualize" it for your food storage – calculate the ingredient quantities you'll need for a whole year. For example, for our family of 4, if they loved the Chicken and Dumplings recipe, and think they'd like it every other week, we'll plan to add 26 times the ingredients to the food store.

Below is an example of "annualizing" a recipe. For this recipe:

Chicken and Dumplings, serves 8
2 pints canned chicken
2 Cans Chicken broth, or 4 Cups chicken bouillon
½ Cup Carrots, dry and rehydrated
½ Cup Onion, diced, dry and rehydrated
½ Cup Peas, dry and rehydrated
4 Cups Flour
1 ½ tsp. Salt
½ Cup shortening
1 ½ cup Water

Because this recipe serves 8 and we are planning for 4, we'll plan to make a half-recipe 26 times to serve it every two weeks, so we'll multiply it by 13. That means we need:

- 26 Pints of canned chicken
- 26 Cans of chicken stock
- 13 Cups of carrots – there are about 12 cups of carrots in a #10 can, so we need about 1.1 Cans or carrots.
- 13 Cups of onions – there are about 12 cups of onions in a #10 can, so we need 1.1 cans
- 13 Cups of peas – there are about 10 cups of peas in a # 10 can, so we need 1.3 cans
- 52 Cups of flour – there are about 12 cups of flour in a #10 can of flour, so we need 4 ⅓ cans of flour. Now if you are grinding your own flour, 1 cup of wheat berries yields 1 ½ to 2 cups of flour (the weight is the same, but the volume increases with grinding.) A #10 can of wheat holds 12 cups of wheat, which would equal 18 Cups of flour, we'd need 2.8 cans of wheat. I'd round up to 3.
- 1 ½ tsp. of salt times 13 equals 19.5 teaspoons, so 6.5 Tablespoons, or about ¾ Cup.
- 6 ½ Cups of shortening. A #10 can of Crisco holds 13.3 Cups, so about half a can of Crisco.

Ideally you compile a list of all the ingredients needed for all the recipes you chose, and run through the calculations once, totally the quantities for each item and adjusting the need column in your inventory accordingly.

An excel spreadsheet is a great way to store your inventory and calculate ingredient totals. My spreadsheet has a tab for inventories, and tabs for recipes. When I add a recipe, I "annualize" it, and add it to the totals for my rotation pantry.

7

Calculating Yields

Use the table below to help translate your chosen recipes into specific lists of what you'll need.

ITEM	EQUIVALENCE
Apple Slices	10 Cups in a #10 Can =1 ¼ lbs. 1 c. dry + 1/2 c. water = 2 c. fresh
Baking Powder	59 Tbs =1 lb
Baking Soda	38 Tbs = 1 lb
Beans	10 Cups in a #10 Can 2 ½ C. Beans = 1 lb 1 lb. beans = 6 lbs. cooked 20 lbs. = 5 gallon bucket = 50 Cups
Carrots	12 Cups in a #10 Can ½ cup dry = 1 cup rehydrated
Celery	2 oz. = 1 Cup 12 Cups in a #10 Can ½ cup dry – 1 cup rehydrated
Cheese Powder	4 cups per lb. 10 Cups in a #10 can 96 Tbs. = 1 lb.

ITEM	EQUIVALENCE
Cocoa	90 Tbs. = 1 lb. 12 Cups in #10 Can = 56 1 cup servings
Corn Meal	4 cups = 1 lb. 11 ¾ Cups in a #10 Can
Corn starch	45 Tbs. = 1 lb. 12 ¾ Cups per #10 Can
Crisco	227 Tbs. = 6 lb. Can 17 Tbs. = 1 Cup 2 ¼ Cup = 1 lb. 13 1/3 Cups of Crisco in a 6 lb. Can 1 c. Crisco + 6 tsp. water =1 c. "butter equivalent"
Eggs – powdered	32 eggs = 1 lb. 2 eggs = 1 oz. = 2 Tb.
Flour	12 Cups in a #10 Can
Honey	20 Tbs. = 1 Cup 6 Cups = 1 lb. 60 lbs. = 5 gallon bucket
Macaroni	12 Cups in a #10 can 2 Cups dry = 5 Cups cooked 18 lbs. = 5 gallon bucket
Meat	1 pint = 1 lb. 1 quart = 2 lbs.
Milk	12 ¾ Cups in a #10 Can = 58 Cups liquid 25 lbs. = 5 gallon bucket = 483 Cups liquid
Mushrooms	4 Cups dry = 3 oz. 20 Cups dry = 1 lb.

ITEM	EQUIVALENCE
Noodles	4 Cups = 8 oz. = 2 ½ Cups cooked
Oats (regular)	12 Cups in #10 Can 1 Cup = 4 oz. 16.5 lbs. = 5 gallon bucket
Onion	1 onion = ½ Cup dry 1 Cup fresh = ⅓ Cup dry 12 Cups in #10 Can
Parsley	30 Tbs. dry = 1 oz.
Pepper	6 Tbs. = 1 oz.
Popcorn	12 Cups in #10 Can 1 Cup = 16 Cups popped
Potato Pearls	12 Cups in #10 Can 4.5 oz. = 1 Cup dry = 2 ½ Cups cooked
Pudding Mix	12.75 Cups in #10 Can
Raisins	4 Cups = 1 lb.
Rice	12 Cups in #10 Can 2 1/3 Cups = 1 lb. 1 Cup dry = 3 Cups cooked 32 lbs. = 5 gallon
Salt	1 ½ Tbs. = 1 oz. 26 oz. box = 39 Tbs. = 117 tsp.
Seasoning Salt	2 Tbs. = 1 oz.
Soup base	1/8 lb. = 9 Cups stock 1 lb. dry = 4-5 Gal liquid
Spices	1 Cup = 16 Tbs. 1 lb. = 64 Tbs.
Sugar	12 Cups in #10 Can 1 lb. = 32 Tbs. = 96 tsp. 40 lbs. = 5 gallon bucket
Sugar, brown	1 1/3 Cups = 1 lb.

ITEM	EQUIVALENCE
Tomato powder	1 Cup powder + 2 Cups water = 2 Cups sauce
Wheat	#10 can = 5.8 lbs. = 12 Cups #10 can = 19 ½ Cups flour 1 Cup of wheat = 1 ½ - 2 Cups flour 1 lb. wheat = 2 ¼ Cup wheat = 3.37 Cups flour 50 lbs. = 5 gallon bucket 100 lbs. = 18 #10 Cans = 3 cases
Yeast	8 oz. = 24 Tbs.

Conversions

If you do your own annualized calculations to convert recipes into annual ingredient quantities, it is helpful to know the following:

- There are 3 Tsp. in a TB.
- There are 4 TB. in ¼ cup, 16 TB. in a cup, 32 in a pint, 64 in a quart and 256 in a Gallon. One TB. is half an ounce.
- There are 2 ounces in ¼ cup, 4 ounces in a ½ cup, 6 ounces in ¾ cup and 8 ounces in a cup.
- There are 2 cups in a pint (16 ounces), 2 pints in a quart (32 ounces), and 4 quarts in a gallon (128 ounces).
- A pint is roughly equivalent to a pound. (A pint's a pound the world around.)
- A serving of protein is generally ¼ to ⅓ lb. (4 to 6 ounces).

Tip:

You can calculate the exact number of calories needed by using an online calculator. Generally speaking, people need between 3000 and 1500 calories per day depending on age, gender, weight and activity level.

- An average 6' 200 lb. man may require 2900 calories per day.
- A 5'7" 145 lb. woman may need about 2000 calories per day.
- A teenage boy 5'4" 120 lbs. may need 2100 calories per day.
- A 13 year old girl 4'9" 95 lbs. may need about 1800 calories per day.

8

Organization

It is important to keep a notebook(s) with all of your recipes and your inventory handy. When the power is out, there's a bit of a panic, and your family is hungry, is not the time to go hunting for a cookbook. It is also helpful to keep all your preparedness books in one place so they can easily be found. Gardening books as well as first aid books will be helpful to have too.

I keep a notebook which contains all the recipes I have planned for use. (I have included them here in the recipe section.) I also keep my list of ingredients which I have annualized based on the number of times I plan to make each recipe. I keep an inventory sheet for monitoring my rotation pantry for replenishment. I also track the number of prepackaged meals in bags (my own homemade MRSs) and bags of bread kits I have on hand.

It's also important to have a stock of flashlights, batteries and candles in an easily accessible location.

It is also a good idea to keep 72 hour emergency backpacks for each family member, also called bug out bags. They should contain, at a minimum, food and water for 72 hours, comfortable shoes and socks, a jacket, flashlight, emergency blanket, maps and a mini first aid kit. Also include any needed prescriptions, inhalers, etc. Consider also including contact information, telephone numbers and important addresses for immediate and extended family members. This will facilitate communication after an emergency. Sometimes it is not possible to reach people in an effected area, but it may be possible to reach relatives further away from the scene of a disaster. Delegate someone to be a contact person.

9

Adapting Your Recipes

Dehydrated vegetables differ in the proportion of dry to use to yield the same amount of fresh vegetables. Most vegetable measurements need to be reduced by half to account for expansion in rehydration.

Onions need to be reduced between a third to a half of the quantity called for in a recipe with fresh ingredients. The onion flavor fades a bit in dehydration, if you want to match the level of flavor, go with replacing by half, if you want to replicate the volume of onion in proportion to other ingredients, replace dry onion by one third the amount of fresh onion.

Milk and eggs can be replaced by their powdered equivalents, rehydrated. Cream can be replaced by evaporated milk.

Fresh cheeses can be replaced by dehydrated cheese, Parmesan, Velveeta or canned cheese. "Process Cheese Foods" are shelf stable and include Laughing Cow cheese and Velveeta. A good compromise in a cheese sauce is to use a "cheese food" for the creaminess of cheese, and bolster the cheesy tang with a bit of cheese powder.

If cheese is in short supply and your casserole recipe calls for topping it with grated cheese, you can replace some or all of the cheese with buttered bread crumbs, perhaps with some Parmesan cheese mixed in. This replaces the crispy, salty contrasting texture of the topping and uses less cheese.

Fresh meats and seafood can be replaced by their canned equivalents, substituting 1 pint canned for every pound of fresh meat. Some meats are considered to be shelf stable such as canned Spam, dry salami, sopressata, Spanish chorizo, and country ham, which are hung and dry cured without refrigeration. Be sure to read the labels to insure the products you use are truly shelf stable.

When cooking your new recipes, be sure to allow time for the dehydrated vegetables to return to their rehydrated state, and if then cooking them in fat, be cautious of splattering. Also, add seasonings late in the process as salt and sugar retard rehydration.

The water used to rehydrate vegetables is very flavorful and can be used in place of water or stock to add flavor to your dishes.

A really good approach is to utilize slow cooking and braising methods to allow foods a long, slow cook time to rehydrate and become very tender. If you are cooking a soup or stew low and slow, you can add your dehydrated vegetables and let them reconstitute in the soup.

Skills to Practice

- Bread Baking
- Canning
  - Dry Pack
  - Water Bath
  - Pressure
- Cooking with Dehydrated Food
- Sprouting seeds
- Cooking in a Dutch oven
- Cooking over a rocket stove
- Cooking in a camp oven
- Starting plants from seeds
- Gardening

Tip:

In case of emergency, I think morale will be very important. One thing I plan for the morale of my family is special treats.

- Roasted marshmallows and s'mores
- Birthday cake on your birthday
- Brownies, warm from the oven
- Fresh bread, butter and homemade jam
- Bacon, sausage and ham
- Chocolate
- Candy, gum and mints
- Apple pie, or rustic baked apples in a lovely, flaky pie crust sprinkled with sugar and cinnamon.

There will be a lot of work to be done, and a lot of effort to maintain good attitudes, and I like to acknowledge people's contributions with treats, a hug and a thank you.

Also, gratitude will be important. Give thanks daily. We can at least be thankful that we are all here together.

10

Containers for Food Storage

#10 Cans

Dry packed food in #10 cans (about a gallon) have the advantage of being sealed with oxygen absorbers to remove oxygen and lengthen shelf life, they are easily stackable and have the advantage of having only a small quantity open at a time.

#10 cans can be purchased from LDS canneries by both LDS members and non-members and cost about a dollar for both a can and a lid. #10 cans are light weight, waterproof, impervious to light and rodent and bug proof.

Buckets

Buckets must be food grade, and are great storage, especially for bulk items. They are heavier than #10 cans, are slightly more oxygen penetrable than cans, and can be breached by very determined rodents. Buckets are typically sealed with larger oxygen absorbers and dry ice, and once open, can be resealed with gamma lids. To add an extra layer of protection and to account for the slight increase in oxygen permeability, do plan to use mylar bag inside the bucket. Mylar bags can be sealed with an impulse sealer, or an iron set on the highest heat setting. (Don't use steam.) You can place a yardstick or board wider than the needed seal across the bucket and place the area of the bag to be sealed across the board, and then iron.

Canning Jars (Mason Jars)

Canning jars are perfect for storing home canned meats, fruits and vegetables. They are also the ideal storage for hot cocoa mix (no oxygen absorber is needed - makes the sugar clump).

You can also store dehydrated foods in canning jars. There is an attachment for the vacuum sealer which will allow you to remove the oxygen further lengthening the shelf life of food. Remember to store your jars in a cool, dark place.

Other Plastic Containers

Food can also be stored in empty plastic soda bottles, bakery buckets or use plastic bins to contain mylar bags. Be sure to use only food grade plastic, which will have a symbol with a 2 imbedded in the plastic. If buying, look for "FDA Approved".

Vacuum Bags

Vacuum bags are good for short-term storage of food, but because it is light permeable, vacuum bags should be packaged in #10 cans, mylar bags or buckets for maximized shelf life.

Mylar Bags

Mylar bags are excellent for food storage, but are challenging to vacuum seal. They are impenetrable to light and very difficult to puncture. Mylar bags can easily be sealed with an impulse sealer. To vacuum seal a mylar bag, cut a strip of regular vacuum bag about an inch wide and of a matching size. Slip the strip inside the mylar bag and position it an inch from the outer edge of the mylar mag. Vacuum seal both bags together, and move the sealer and impulse seal just the mylar bag again, one half inch from the edge.

Mason Jars

Mason jars can be used to store pressure canned, water bath canned, and vacuum packed dehydrated foods. Mason jars can be vacuum sealed with a vacuum sealer with a jar attachment.

Tip:

Many bakeries have food grade storage buckets available free for the taking. It might be worth a call to your local bakeries t ask if you may have the, Also some club stores have bakery departments which use tubs of icing, which can be washed and repurposed as free food storage containers.

11

Equipment for Food Storage

Dry Pack Canner

Dry pack canners can be purchased online, or borrowed from the LDS (Church of Jesus Christ of the Latter Day Saints) canneries by LDS members. If you are LDS or have an LDS friend, this is a great way to go. If not, possibly you can locate one on Craigslist, eBay or through Gering and Son at http://www.geringandson.com or via other online retailers.

Since canners are more costly items, it might be a good idea to pool resources with a few like-minded families and share a canner.

Dehydrator

Excalibur dehydrators are widely considered to be the best. Try to pick one up at a garage sale or thrift store. Alternately purchase directly from Excalibur at:

http://www.excaliburdehydrator.com/.

Note: Excalibur sells refurbished dehydrators at a discount.

Food Slicer

A food slicer makes slicing vegetables or meats for dehydrating much faster. It is also much safer than a mandolin.

Grain Mill

A grain mill is a must have if you are storing wheat. Country Living is widely regarded to be the best. It is manually operated, but can easily be converted to electric. The Wonder Mill is also a good choice. Family Grain Mill and Nutrimill are two other good brands. If you plan to grind corn into corn meal and polenta, the Nutrimill is a good choice.

Note: The Family Grain Mill is as highly rated as the Country Living at a fraction of the cost.

Pressure Canner

The best pressure canner is widely regarded to be the All American but there are many good brands. It is important not to have a rubber gasket, which can wear out, and gauges must be checked on used pressure canners before use. Look for them at garage sales and buy the largest you can afford.

Vacuum Sealer

There are several good vacuum sealers available. I use a Weston Pro-2300 which is very robust and seals quickly.

Tip: Vacuum sealers can often be found at thrift stores and garage sales. Keep an eye out for the mason jar sealer attachment too.

Water Bath Canner

Water bath canners are much less expensive than pressure canners and can be found at Walmart, along with canning supplies and jars.

Tip:

Consider banding together with a group of like-minded local people and buying and sharing the equipment you need. It might also be fun to host food storage parties where you seal and can mass volumes of food, spilt the costs and divide the fruits of your labor amongst the group.

12

Supplies for Food Storage

Oxygen Absorbers

Oxygen absorbers can by bought most inexpensively from the LDS cannery and can also be bout online. Try nitro-pak.com. The trick to using oxygen absorbers is to keep the bag sealed as long as possible and co-ordinate your canning or bag sealing to leave the fewest bags exposed to air for the least amount of time possible and to reseal the bag of absorber as soon as possible. This will maintain the life of their functionality for as long as possible.

If you are opening and resealing either mason jars or plastic buckets with gamma lids, you will need to replace the oxygen absorbers periodically. In mason jars, when they fail to open with a pop sound, the oxygen bag needs to be replaced.

Vacuum Sealer Bags

Vacuum sealer bags must be at least 3 mm in thickness. There are several online suppliers. Also Walmart carries a pack of 20 gallon size bags for about $16.You can also buy rolls of vacuum material tubes you can cut to any size and impulse seal both the bottoms and tops to form bags.

Mylar Bags

Mylar bags can be bought most inexpensively from the LDS cannery or from many online sources. There is a trick to sealing mylar bags using a vacuum bag insert, vacuum seal a segment of a vacuum bag inside the opening of a mylar bag. Then move your sealer closer to the end of the bag, beyond the vacuum bag, and seal the mylar again. This is a very effective method of storing food.

Canning Jars and Lids

Walmart is a good source for canning jars and supplies, and they can also be found at many retailers including Ace Hardware stores.

Canning Kit

A canning kit will include a jar lifter, funnels, and a magnetic stick which will help you remove lids from hot water without burning yourself. They are a worthwhile and inexpensive investment.

13

Where to Buy Food to Store

Build Versus Buy

If money isn't a factor, then certainly you can buy prepackaged kits. Do try samples first to insure your family will eat the meals.

If you are interested in getting food storage for the best prices you'll need to do some shopping around. If you are near a LDS cannery, they usually have the best prices for the items they sell. Currently my local cannery sells beans, oats, rice, wheat and flour in #10 cans, pre-packaged and many other things in bulk to can yourself. They also sell #10 cans, lids, boxes, oxygen absorbers, food storage bags and clips. Since the LDS canneries only carry a limited number of items, you'll need to look elsewhere for everything else.

Refer to item specifics in the inventory section below for price comparisons as of the publish date. Your results may vary. Do check prices in your area and if buying online, include shipping and materials in your calculations.

Remember: If you buy commercially packaged food, and are planning to grow your own food, you'll need to be able to dehydrate or can your summer harvest in order to be eating vegetables through the following winter. You may not be able to buy commercially packaged food when what you have is gone.

LDS Cannery

LDS canneries are often the least expensive source of what they carry. They have several items for purchase canned, and also offer bulk bags, #10 cans, lids, boxes, labels and oxygen absorbers. Although they only loan dry pack canners to LDS members, canners can be purchased online and packaging your own food is one of the most economical ways to fill your food storage. I am not a member of the LDS church, but I certainly admire their approach to encouraging preparedness, and a nicer group of people you are unlikely to meet.

LDS Cannery Locations

AK - Palmer
Phone: (907) 746-3509
4350 S Bodenburg Loop Rd
Palmer, Alaska 99645

AZ - Snowflake
Phone: (928) 536-3458
641 South Main #1
Snowflake, Arizona 85937

AZ - Flagstaff
Phone: (928) 527-3713
5021 Empire Ave
Flagstaff, Arizona 86001

AZ - St. Johns
Phone: (928)337-3745
155 East Commercial Street
St. Johns, Arizona 85936

AZ - Mesa
Phone: (480) 214-9114
235 S El Dorado Circle
Mesa, Arizona 85202

AZ - Tucson
Phone: (520) 514-9039
3535 S Richey
Tucson, Arizona 85713

CA - Chico
Phone: (530) 894-8302
1040 Marauder Street
Chico, California 95973

CA - Colton
Phone: (909) 824-1307
791 North Pepper Avenue
Colton, California 92324

CA - Concord
Phone: (925) 798-1763
1063 Detroit Ave
Concord, California 94518

CA - Fountain Valley
Phone: (714) 437-9205
17350 Mount Hermann Cir
Fountain Valley, CA 92708

CA - Fresno
Phone: (559) 255-2377
1425 North Rabe Avenue
Fresno , California 93727

CA - Los Angeles
Phone: (323) 261-6351
2730 East 12th Street
Los Angeles, CA 90023

CA - Sacramento
Phone: (916) 381-5150
8401 24th Avenue
Sacramento, CA 95826

CA - San Diego
Phone: (858) 279-5712
4722 Mercury Street
San Diego, California 92111

CA - Santa Clara
Phone: (408) 986-1872
442 Nelo Street
Santa Clara, CA 95054

CA - Stockton
Phone: (209) 943-1892
3112 Loomis Road
Stockton, California 95205

CA - Sylmar
Phone: (818) 833-6696
15648 Roxford Street
Sylmar, California 91342

CO - Aurora (Denver)
Phone: (303) 371-7650
3233 Fraser Street
Aurora, Colorado 80011

CO - Colorado Springs
Phone: (719) 550-1158
4090 Center Park Dr
Colorado Springs, CO 80916

CO - Grand Junction
Phone: (970) 245-2011
2956 North Ave #2
Grand Junction, CO 81504

HI - Honolulu
Phone: (808) 841-6311
1120 Kalihi Street
Honolulu, Hawaii 96817

ID - Burley
Phone: (208) 678-0434
245 North Overland Dr
Burley, Idaho 83318-0861

ID - Garden City (Boise)
Phone: (208) 375-7893
604 East 46th Street
Garden City, Idaho 83714

ID - Idaho Falls
Phone: (208) 529-2201
770 West Anderson St
Idaho Falls, Idaho 83402

ID - Pocatello
Phone: (208) 233-1937
590 Roosevelt Avenue
Pocatello, Idaho 83201

MN - Apple Valley
Phone: (952) 891-3099
6890 145th Street W
Apple Valley, MN 55124

MO - Bridgeton (St. Louis)
Phone: (314) 344-0313
12843 Pennridge Dr
Bridgeton, Missouri 63044

MO - Kansas City
Phone: (816) 453-2398
3601 NE Kimball Drive
Kansas City, Missouri 64161

MT - Missoula
Phone: (406) 721-3197
6200 Industrial Way
Missoula, Montana 59808

NE - Omaha
Phone: (402) 891-1577
13232 Portal Dr. Ste. 3
Omaha, NE 68138

NM - Albuquerque
Phone: (505) 343-1905
4400 Presidential Dr NE
Albuquerque , NM 87109

NM - Farmington
Phone: (505) 326-3506
925 Cannery Court Ste B
Farmington , NM 87401

NV - Las Vegas
Phone: (702) 631-2438
4455 Allen Ln
North Las Vegas, NV89031

NV - Reno
Phone: (775) 856-2245
580 Reactor Way Ste 1
Reno, Nevada 89502

OK - Oklahoma City
Phone: (405) 692-3883
11224 South Meridian
Oklahoma City, OK 73173

OR - Portland
Phone: (971) 230-0770
10420 SE 82nd Ave
Portland, Oregon 97086

OR - Springfield
Phone: (541) 726-9201
1690 South A St
Springfield, Oregon 97477

OR - St. Paul
Phone: (503) 633-4433
16572 River Road NE
St. Paul, Oregon 97137

OR - White City
Phone: (541) 826-4220
7575 Pacific Ave
White City, Oregon 97503

TX - Austin
Phone: 512-252-2177
3912 Gattis School Rd #104
Round Rock, Texas 78664

TX - Carrollton (Dallas)
Phone: (972) 242-8595
1100 West Jackson Road
Carrollton , Texas 75006

TX - El Paso
Phone: (915) 56601335
2910 Tularosa
El Paso, Texas 79903

TX - Houston
Phone: (281) 537-1786
16333 Hafer Road
Houston, Texas 77090

TX - San Antonio
Phone: (210) 520-1122
6880 Alamo Downs Pkwy
San Antonio, Texas 78238

WA - Bremerton
Phone: (360) 373-6028
288 Wilkes Ave
Bremerton, WA 98132

WA - Kennewick
Phone: (509) 735-6455
6501 W Deschutes
Kennewick, WA 99336

WA - Kent
Phone: (253) 852-8552
1412 West Morton
Kent, WA 98035-0825

WA - Mt. Vernon
Phone: (360) 424-0335
1524 Riverside Drive #14
Mt. Vernon, WA 98273

WA - Mukilteo
Phone: (425) 315-1514
4215 C Russell Road
Mukilteo, WA 98275

WA - Spokane
Phone: (509) 928-1035
E 9423 Fourth Avenue
Spokane Valley, WA 99214

WY - Evanston
Phone: (307) 679-7594
315 Elm Street
Evanston , Wyoming 82930

WY - Green River
Phone: (307) 875-3972
120 Shoshone Drive
Green River, Wyoming
82935

Warehouse Stores

Costco, Sam's Club, Cash and Carry, and BJ's Wholesale club are great sources of food for canning and long term storage. The large quantities you can buy are very economical for long term storage. Buy case packs of chicken breasts, turkey, beef or pork and can them. This will fill your larder and you can take advantage of the big-buy prices for everyday eating as you eat and replenish your rotation pantry.

Costco.com sells Shelf-Reliance and other freeze-dried food packages. They also sell a few can rotation systems.

I prefer the business Costco for buying fresh produce, because they carry large bags of washed and cut vegetables ready for the dehydrator. I prefer the regular Costco for buying canned goods, because the business Costco sells canned goods in #10 cans, and a gallon of tomato sauce, for example, is too much for my family to use regularly.

Big Box Stores

Walmart carries dehydrated and bulk food items and has very good prices. It is also a very good source of sundries, batteries and other supplies at good prices.

Specialty Suppliers

There are many online suppliers of special dehydrated food intended for long-term storage. Honeyville, Shelf-Reliance, Mountain House, Wise Foods, and Walton Feed are great places to shop. Do include the cost of shipping in your calculation of which is the best value for you.

Farmers Markets and Other Seasonal Sources

Farmers markets and other seasonal markets are a great way to buy large quantities of the very nicest fruits and vegetables to dehydrate and store. You might consider a drive out to your nearest farming community and speak to the farmers themselves. I grew up in a farming area and it was always possible to buy fruit straight from the farmer, especial fruit which was too ripe for shipping to market. It was the best tasting and the cheapest by far.

Here are a few seasonal ideas:

January
Look for avocados, bananas, cabbage, cauliflower, citrus, mushrooms, pears, turnips and squash.

February
In season are avocados, bananas, broccoli, cabbage, cauliflower, citrus, mango, mushrooms, pears, turnips and squash.

March
Good buys are artichokes, asparagus, avocados, bananas, broccoli, citrus, grapefruit, mushrooms, pears, turnips, radishes and spinach.

April
Look for asparagus, bananas, cabbage, citrus, onion, pineapple, radishes, spinach and strawberries.

May

Look for deals on asparagus, bananas, celery, onion, papayas, peas, pineapple, potatoes, strawberries and tomatoes.

June

So much in season. Find avocados, apricots, bananas, cantaloupe, cherries, corn, cucumber, green beans, limes, mangos, nectarines, onion, peaches, peas, peppers, pineapple, plums, and summer squash.

July

Think about apricots, bananas, blueberries, cantaloupe, cherries, corn, cucumber, dill, green beans, limes, mangos, nectarines, onion, peaches, peas, peppers, pineapple, plums, and summer squash.

August

Look for apples, bananas, beets, berries, cabbage, cabbage, carrots, corn, cucumber, dill, figs, melon, nectarines, peaches, peas, peppers, plums, potatoes, summer squash and tomatoes.

September

There should be deals on apples, bananas, beets, berries, cabbage, cabbage, carrots, corn, cucumber, dill, figs, melon, nectarines, peaches, peas, peppers, plums, potatoes, summer squash and tomatoes.

October

Look for good buys on apples, bananas, broccoli, grapes, peppers, pumpkin, and yams.

November

Look for good buys on apples, bananas, broccoli, cabbage, cauliflower, cranberries, mushrooms, pumpkin, and sweet potatoes.

December

In season are apples, avocados, bananas, citrus, mushrooms, pumpkin, pears, pineapple and tangerines.

Food Co-ops

Food co-ops can be a great source of low-cost, healthy food. Check the phone book or internet for co-ops in your area. Most will let you shop without becoming a member, but will offer a discount to members after a fee. Do the math and determine if you will be spending enough with them to justify the cost of membership with the discounts you will receive.

My local co-op costs $100 annually to belong, and offers 10% discounts regularly with 15% discount periodically (monthly) and will offer a 20% discount if you volunteer to work there. You'd need to spend $800 - $1000 annually to justify the cost of membership.

14

How to Dehydrate Food

Dehydrating food is really easy. Most foods you simply spread on the dehydrator trays, set the temperature to 120°, and leave it for several hours. You cannot "over dry" a food, so unlike cooking, you can leave the dehydrator running for a few hours over the recommended drying time with no ill effects on the food.

Potatoes, sweet potatoes and yams need to be cooked first. Cook them until just barely tender, cool, peel, and then slice or dice to dry. You can also press to mash sweet potatoes with your hand and then simply dehydrate the pile. It's easiest if you mash them on the dehydrator tray so you don't have to transfer them while wet. Citrus fruits are sliced thin and then dried.

To test for dryness, bend the food items. Most foods should snap or break when bent.

When you are ready to unload the dehydrator, have zip-lock bags or vacuum bags ready to load your food into. Leaving the food exposed to air will cause it to draw moisture from the air. If this happens you can simply dehydrate again.

You can place an open gallon-size zip-lock bag inside a #10 can and fold the top down around the edge of the can. This will hold the bag steady, upright and open for filling. The Excalibur dehydrators come with removable tray liners which you can curl up and upend directly into the can.

When unloading, avoid contact with the front panel, or sides of the dehydrator, because they may have some condensation and remoisten your food. As soon as possible, vacuum seal or dry pack your dehydrated food into mylar bags or #10 cans to prevent exposure to light which shortens the shelf life of your food.

Speed tip: Costco Business centers sell produce already cut up which can go straight onto the dehydrator tray, which is quite a time savings.

Case Hardening

Case hardening happens when the outside of a food dries leaving the interior moist which leads to spoilage. This can be prevented by dehydrating at no more than 120°. This insures the interior of the food dries too.

Dehydrating Fruit

Food	Preparation	Drying Time	Yield
All Fruit Very thinly sliced	Peel and slice	10 – 12 hours	5 - 7 lbs. = 1 #10 can
Sliced fruit ¼"		12-15 hours	5-7 lbs. = 1 #10 can
Fruit Rollup	Cook and puree fruit, spread on plastic over tray	15-20 hours	
Apples	Peel, slice	12-15 hours	6.75 lbs. = 1 #10 can
Blueberries	Wash and dry gently	18-20 hours	
Citrus	Slice paper thin	15-20 hours	5-6 lemons = 1 #10 can
Grapes	Wash	15-20 hours	
Nectarines	Peel, slice	12-15 hours	
Prunes	Whole	48 hours	
Peaches			
Pears	Peel, slice	12-15 hours	6.75 lbs. = 1 #10 can
Plums	Peel, slice	12-15 hours	
Rhubarb	Slice	12-15 hours	

Dehydrating Vegetables

Food	Preparation	Drying Time	Yield
Asparagus	Wash an cut into 1" pieces	5-6 hours	
Beets	Steam or bake until tender. Cool, peel, and slice or dice.	8-12 hours	
Broccoli	Wash and cut into florets	10-14 hours or until brittle	3 lbs. = 1 #10 can
Cabbage	Wash, trim and cut into 1/8" strips	7-11 hours	1 lb. = 1 #10 can
Carrots	Wash, peel, slice or dice.	6 – 10 hours	
Celery	Dice	3 – 10 hours	15 lbs. = 1 #10 can
Corn	Cook and remove from cob. OR use frozen straight from the bag.	12 – 15 hours	15 lbs. (frozen) = 1 #10 can
Green Beans	Wash, snap ends, cut into 1" pieces	8-12 hours	
Onions	Slice or dice (do these outside due to odor.)		
Mushrooms	Wipe lean, slice (wet mushrooms discolor)	10 hours or until brittle	5 lbs. = 1 #10 can
Potato Pearls/diced	Cook, peel, dice		
Potato shreds	Dehydrate straight from frozen		
Potato flakes			

Food	Preparation	Drying Time	Yield
Tomato powder	Wash, slice tomatoes	12 – 15 hours	
Spinach	Wash, stem		1 lb. – 1 #10 can

Dehydrating Meat

Evenly slice partially frozen (to ease cutting) beef or other meat. Choose cuts with very little fat and slice (or have your butcher slice) about ¼" thick. Marinate or rub the meat with seasonings of your choice, and lay in a single layer and dry at 150° for about 4 – 6 hours or until jerky cracks when bent, but doesn't break. The drier you make your jerky, the longer it will last. Jerky can be vacuum sealed and stored in mylar bags or mason jars, but only has a published shelf life of about a year.

Dehydrating Fish

Fish jerky is challenging to make. It must be fresh enough to prevent spoilage during the drying time, and oily fish goes rancid quickly.

Dehydrating Cheese

Cheese can be dehydrated and turned into cheese powder. Line the drying trays with paper towels and change out the paper towels periodically as they absorb the oil release by the cheese during drying. Dry at the lowest temperature possible until completely crisp. Dry cheese can be powdered in a blender, spice or coffee blender or food mill. Can or seal with an oxygen absorber and keep in a cool dark place.

How to Rehydrate Dehydrated Food

For most dehydrated foods, place in a bowl, cover with hot water and let sit 20 minutes. By volume, add about 3 parts water for 1 part food. You can also use cool water, but the process may take 3 or 4 hours, and the food should be kept refrigerated. Avoid salting (or adding sugar) to food before it is fully rehydrated, because salt and sugar slow the rehydration process. Save the water used to rehydrate and add it to your recipe in the place of water or stock.

Food tends to rehydrate closest to its original form when the food was firmer to start with. For example, apples, pear and onions rehydrate back closer to their original for whereas bananas and tomatoes do not. In the case of bananas and tomatoes, they do transform into something good. Bananas are delicious treats in their dry form, and tomatoes transform into a powder which can be reconstituted to tomato paste or tomato juice.

When a recipe called for food to be rehydrated, and also calls for water or stock, use the soaking liquid to replace all or part of the stock the recipe call for. Both nutrients and flavor will be in that water and we don't want to waste it.

15

Canning

One of the best ways to package food for long term storage is canning, but there are multiple types of canning. Here are some descriptions to clarify.

Dry Pack Canning

Dry pack canning is the act of sealing dry food into cans, typically #10 cans

Dry Packing in Buckets

You can also dry pack into buckets, typically 5 or 6 gallon buckets. Oxygen absorbers are used here too. Buckets stack well and can be reused for many things. Once opened, they can be reclosed with oxygen packs and gamma lids which screw on and can be resealed over and over. Dry ice is sometimes used to evacuate air from the bucket just prior to sealing.

The disadvantage to buckets is that they are slightly oxygen permeable, unlike cans, and they require opening a larger volume of food at once. Of course you can reseal them, but opening and closing buckets causes the oxygen absorber to wear out and it will need to be replaced. We use 5 gallon buckets to store dog food.

Many people use buckets for deep larder storage and many companies sell filled buckets of commercially available dry foods this way. Commercially shipping buckets is costly, and buckets are more costly to buy than the equivalent number of #10 cans.

Water Bath Canning

Water bath canning is used to store high-acid fruits, jams and jellies into mason jars for long term storage.

Pressure Canning

Pressure canning is used to "put up" meats, fish, vegetables, dairy and other (not high-acid) foods for long term storage. Pressure canned foods are considered safe for at least two years, and have historically been eaten after far longer storage. Pressure canning is very important if you plan to serve meat and fish. Commercially canned meat products such as spam and Vienna sausage cannot compare to home canned meatballs, sausages, pulled pork, bbq beef and taco fillings.

Water Bath Canning Details

Water bath canning is recommended for high acids foods such as apples, applesauce, jellies, jams and tomatoes. Water bath canning involves filling sterile jars with food, wiping the rims, applying lids and rims and then placing in a canning pot or other pot with a rack in the bottom to prevent the jars from touching the bottom of the pan.

Water bath canners must have enough room for the jars to be covered by water by 1 to 2 inches above the tops of the jars. If the jars don't fill the pot and there is room for a jar to tip over, empty jars with some water added can be place holders to keep jars upright.

Processing guidelines are below, which may have changed, so please verify the time and pressure recommendations with current USDA guidelines.

Water Bath Canning Processing Times

	Style of pack	Jar size	Water Bath (minutes)	Pressure canner (minutes)
Apples, sliced	Hot	Pint	20	8
		Quart	20	8
Applesauce	Hot	Pint	15	8
		Quart	20	10
Berries	Hot	Pint	15	8
		Quart	15	8
	Raw	Pint	15	8
		Quart	20	10
Cherries	Hot	Pint	15	8
		Quart	20	10
	Raw	Pint	25	10
		Quart	25	10
Fruit juices	Hot	Pint	5	NR
		Quart	5	NR
		Half-gallon	10	NR
Peaches	Hot	Pint	20	10
		Quart	25	10

Pressure Canning Details

Pressure canning requires the ability to read and follow directions well. Failure to do so could threaten your family's health. Please follow all directions carefully and follow current USDA guidelines for proper timing and procedures.

When pressure canning, choose from the allowable sized jars, and determine whether the food can be canned raw or must be hot packed after cooking until two thirds done. Place food in sterile jars leaving the require amount of head space (either 1" or 1 ½ ").

Wipe the top rims of the jars clean. Place lids and rims on and finger tighten. Heat a few inches(about a gallon) of water in your pressure canner until hot and steaming. Add the jars one at a time on top of the racks so the jars are not sitting on the bottom of the canner.

Close the canner according to manufacturers' directions. Heat the canner until it begins to steadily vent off steam. Set a timer for 10 minutes and wait for the 10 minutes to elapse, which will give time for the air to be vented from the canner.

Place the correct weight on top of the canner, wait for it to come up to the proscribed pressure, and begin timing according to the times listed for the food you are canning and the size jar you are using.

After the time has elapsed, turn the heat off and allow the canner to cool. Once cool enough to touch, remove jars to a towel on the counter and allow to cool completely. Once cooled completely, check the seals. If properly sealed, the jars may be stored. Use any unsuccessfully sealed jars shortly and refrigerate.

Please refer to current guidelines. The list below was current only at the time of writing and current best practices may have subsequently changed. Please follow current USDA recommendations.

Pressure Canning Processing Times - Vegetables

Minutes to Process			
Vegetables	Raw or Hot	Pints	Quarts
Asparagus, spears or pieces	Either	30	40
Beans or peas, shelled, dried	Hot	75	90
Beans, baked or Beans, dry, with tomato or molasses sauce	Hot	65	75
Beans, fresh lima—shelled	Either	40	50
Beans, snap and Italian—pieces	Either	20	25
Beets, whole, cubed, or sliced	Hot	25	30
Carrots, sliced or diced	Either	25	30
Corn, cream style	Hot	85	No
Corn, whole kernel	Either	55	85
Mixed vegetables	Hot	75	90
Mushrooms, whole or sliced, hot pack (½ pint same as pint) NOTE: Wild mushrooms cannot be canned safely.	Hot	45	No
Peas, green or English, shelled	Either	40	40
Peppers (½ pint same as pint)	Hot	35	No
Potatoes, sweet, pieces or whole	Hot	65	90
Potatoes, white, cubed or whole	Hot	35	40
Continued on next page.			
Pumpkin and winter squash,	Hot	55	90

Minutes to Process			
Vegetables	**Raw or Hot**	**Pints**	**Quarts**
cubed			
Spinach and other greens	Hot	70	90
Succotash	Hot	60	85

Pressure Canning Processing Times - Meats

Minutes to Process			
Proteins	**Hot or Raw**	**Pints**	**Quarts**
Chicken or rabbit, cut up, without bones	Either	70	90
Chicken or rabbit, cut up, with bones	Either	65	75
Ground meat	Hot	75	90
Chopped meat	Either	75	90
Strips, cubes or chunks of meat	Either	75	90
Meat stock (broth)	Hot	20	25
Fish	Raw	100	No
Smoked fish		110	No
Shrimp (cover in salted water)	Either	45	No

Pressure Canning Steps to Determine Time and Pressure

1. Determine whether to pack raw or whether food must be cooked through and hot.
2. Follow directions for headspace. (NOTE: Head space is 1 inch for vegetables and all meats except chicken and rabbit, which is 1½ inch.)
3. Determine processing time.
4. Determine pressure based on elevation for either dial or weighted gauge pressure.

    a. Dial Gauge Canner:

Altitude	Pressure
2000-4000 feet	12
4000-6000 feet	13
6000-8000 feet	14

    b. Weighted Gauge Canner: Use 15 lbs. for all

Tip:

When considering whether to hot pack or raw pack meats and seafood, you might experiment with each. Sometimes, surprisingly, cooked or par-cooked meats and seafood can better than their raw versions, resulting in better finished textures. Also, brining can result in better flavors and textures.

Tip:

In a long-term disaster scenario, you will need a garden to grow your own vegetables. Even if you buy your dehydrated food pre-packaged now, you will need to learn to can or root cellar in order to have vegetables through the winter when your pre-packaged supplies run out.

16

Cooking Without Electricity

Grilling

Your gas grill is a great short term cooking solution while you have propane, and charcoal will work thereafter. Of course wood can be substituted from charcoal.

Rocket Stoves

A rocket stove uses venturi action to produce high heat cooking fires with very little fuel, typically sticks or small branches. It can be constructed from tin cans, and it very cost effective to run. They can also be bought online; Google "rocket stove". Stovetek makes great rocket stoves for about $100, approximately, depending on the options you select.
See http://www.stovetec.net/us/index.php.

Wonder Ovens

A wonder oven looks like a bean bag chair in a cube shape, or a small bean bag chair in a large plastic bin. Food is heated to boiling and then nestled into the bean bag and covered. The wonder oven insulates so well the food cooks on the residual heat. It is somewhat like a slow cooker, although wonder oven cooking takes about twice as long as a slow cooker. This pairs well with a rocket stove as you can heat a pot of water to boiling, add your dehydrated ingredients, and stash it in the wonder oven to slow cook all day. Wonder ovens can be made or bought depending on your skill and patience with polystyrene balls. Google "wonder oven". They are about $50 online.

It is possible to bake bread in a wonder oven. The bread dough is placed in a can, covered and placed into a pot with water which is brought to a boil. The whole assembly is then placed in the wonder oven to finish cooking. Once cooled, the bread can be removed from the can and sliced into lovely, round slices, perfect for sandwiches. The cans used for baking bread are the large-size juice cans commonly filled with V8 or pineapple juice at the store.

Solar Ovens

Solar ovens are fantastic for cooking when the sun is shining regardless of whether it is cold or hot outside. The oven must be position (and repositioned) to continually face the sun. Solar ovens range from $200 - $300. One brand to consider is the GLOBAL sun oven

Brick Oven

It's possible to build an oven from bricks, into a cube or dome with an opening in front. A fire is built inside, and a long peel (big, long spatula) is used to place and remove food in the oven. This is how wood-fired pizza is made, and once you master the fine art of wood-fired cooking, you'll surely be drawing crowds for your wonderful food!

Dutch Ovens

Dutch ovens have been used for generations in America and were the most often used method for chuck wagon trail cooking as well as hearth cooking for settlers and beyond. Dutch ovens are very versatile, allowing baking, braising (slow cooking), roasting, frying or boiling. Dutch ovens are built to allow placement among the coals of a fire, and also to allow coals to be stacked on top of the lid of the pot. You can also use the lid as a griddle.

To bake, 3/4ths of the coals are placed on top of the oven, ¼ th below.
To Roast, the coals are half on top of the pot, half below.
To simmer the coals are 3/4ths below and 1/4th above.
To boil or fry all the coals are below the pot.

To cook successfully in a Dutch oven, one must learn to gauge the temperature of the pot. Without a thermometer, the best way to do this is to hold your hand at the even with the top of the pot with the lid off and count the seconds for how long you can keep your hand in place before the heat is intolerable.

Seconds of heat tolerance and estimated temperature:

1 second	500 degrees
2 seconds	450 degrees
3 seconds	400 degrees
4 seconds	350 degrees
5 seconds	300 degrees
6 seconds	250 degrees
7 seconds	200 degrees

Alternately, you can aim an infrared thermometer at the side of the pot. Infrared thermometers range in price from $20 to $40.

If you place a ring of 18 briquettes around the top of a 12" Dutch Oven and 6 below, you'll be baking at about 350 degrees. 14 above and 10 below will roast at 350 degrees. 6 above and 18 below will simmer and all 24 below will be perfect for boiling or frying.

Size up or down the number of briquettes for larger or smaller ovens. Also ovens can be stacked allowing the upper coals for lower pots to server as the bottom coals for the pot stacked on top.

In addition to the Dutch Oven itself, you'll need a pot lifter. Be sure to keep children away from the hot pot.

Camp Ovens

Coleman makes a compact camp oven, which is about 1 square foot in size, and costs about $40. It works beautifully paired with a rocket stove and can bake small loaves of bread, or any other baked goods in pans less than 12" in any direction. Practice using this in a non-emergency situation so you'll know how it works.

Cooling Without Electricity

It is possible to store food at near refrigeration temperatures in a root cellar. If you don't have one, they are pretty easy to make. You can dig a hole to use, put some rocks in the bottom, and line it with weed cloth (to keep pests out). Layer in vegetables in layers separated by moist sawdust and the vegetables should keep in there as they would in your refrigerator. Alternately you can bury a large box, clay pot or galvanized trash can with lid. You need to make sure rain water won't flood your root cellar. Plan to shape the dirt around so rain is channeled away. If you container doesn't have a lid, cover it with a board and weight it down.

Other items which would keep well in a root cellar include cured meats like country ham and salami, as well as canned cheese. Washington State University (WSU) makes a canned, real cheese called Cougar Gold. It's delicious. It is canned, and lasts well under refrigeration. I think it would be interesting to conduct an experiment to see how well it would last in a root cellar.

Meats and cheeses do prefer less humidity in storage than fruits and vegetables. In a classic root cellar, these are best stored on a high shelf. Items like carrots prefer higher humidity, and would do well to have the sawdust around them moistened periodically.

Tip:

Declare a weekend to be "power free" and have your whole family give up their modern conveniences and cook meals with solar heat, or over a campfire. Pick a lovely summer evening and enjoy your time together.

17

Water

Plan to store at least 3 gallons per person per day for an initial period, and plan to have access to much more should you need it. If you live in a rainy climate, you can gather water from your downspouts. You will likely need a another source from a nearby lake or stream. Plan to be able to filter and purify water, and/or to be able to pasteurize it by heating to 149 degrees for a few minutes. Large plastic tanks called Intermediate Bulk Containers are a good, low cost way to store hundreds of gallons, but you should also have more portable means to store available in case you need to relocate.

A good water filtration system is an excellent investment. Alternately you can build one of your own using commercially produced filters. Go online and research Katadyn and Berkey filters.

Tip:

In case of emergency, there are several sources of water around your home - the pool, Jacuzzi and water heater to name a few.

We live in a rainy climate and can capture runoff from the roof into tanks which fit under the deck. This way there is no unsightly tank in the yard, but we are secure knowing we have plenty of water on hand.

18

Inventories

Deep Larder

Note: the prices listed were current local prices at the time of writing. Your experience may vary.

Item	Type	Shelf Life in years	Lbs. per person	Price Comparisons Per pound DIY = self-pack
Baking				
Baking soda		forever		$.54 ClubCo - DIY
Salt	Sea salt	forever	10	$.18 ClubCo - DIY
Sugar (total)			**60**	
Sugar	white sugar	30+		$.68 ClubCo - DIY $.60 LDS – DIY $1.03 BoxMart
Sugar	brown sugar	30+		$.78 ClubCo - DIY
Sugar	powder	30+		$.74 ClubCo - DIY
Sugar	honey	30+		$2.48 ClubCo
Sugar	Honey powder	30+		$3.59 BoxMart
Beans			**75**	

Item	Type	Shelf Life in years	Lbs. per person	Price Comparisons Per pound DIY = self-pack
Beans	Black	30		$.67 LDS - DIY $.83 ClubCo - DIY $3.00 Online
Beans	Pinto	30		$.67 LDS - DIY $.88 ClubCo - DIY $2.78 Online
Beans	White	30		$.64 LDS - DIY $2.04 Online
Beans	Lentils	20		$.67 ClubCo - DIY $1.64 Online DIY
Beans	Garbanzo	30		$1.03 ClubCo - DIY $1.91 Online DIY
Condiments				
Vinegar		forever		
Dairy				
Milk	powder	20	60	
Butter-milk	Powder			$16.17 BoxMart
Eggs	powder	15	2 cans	$10.66 BoxMart
Cheese - Cheddar	powder	15		$5.33 BoxMart $9.54 Online
Fats			**96**	**Per lb.**
Butter	Canned	5		
Butter	powder	15		$19.98 BoxMart $21.49 Online
Margarine	Powder			$13.19 BoxMart $15.19 Online
Coconut oil		5		$3.00 BoxMart
Olive oil		4		$1.66 ClubCo

Item	Type	Shelf Life in years	Lbs. per person	Price Comparisons Per pound DIY = self-pack
Fruit				**Prices per can**
Apple		30		$5.70 LDS – DIY $15.57 BoxMart $22.29 Online
Apricot		5		$18.25 BoxMart 25.19 Online
Banana		5		$8.73 BoxMart $10.39 Online
Blueberry		5		$26.64 BoxMart $32.39 Online
Cranberry		5		$.25 ClubCo DIY
Lemons		5		$.77 per lb. ClubCo DIY
Oranges		5		
Pineapple		5		$27.68 BoxMart $29.69 Online
Raspberry		5		$20.57 BoxMart $24.69 Online
Grains				**Prices per pound**
Corn	popcorn	12		$.89 Online DIY
Corn	dried			$13.87 BoxMart
Cornmeal				$.85 BoxMart
Oats (Total)			**25**	
Oats	Quick oats	30		$.64 LDS DIY $4.00 Online
Oats	Regular	30		$.61 LDY DIY $3.86 Online
Rice	**white**	**30**	**40**	$.52 LDS DIY $50 ClubCo DIY $2.40 Online

Item	Type	Shelf Life in years	Lbs. per person	Price Comparisons Per pound DIY = self-pack
Quinoa	quinoa	8		$2.37 ClubCo DIY
Wheat			**220**	
Wheat	hard red	30+		$.46 LDS DIY $2.26 Online
Wheat	white	30+		$.46 LDS DIY $2.29 Online
Wheat	flour	10		$.71 LDS $.29 ClubCo DIY $.94 Online DIY
Wheat	cream of wheat	15		$2.21 ClubCo
Wheat	pasta - spaghetti	30		$.96 LDS $1.24 ClubCo
Wheat	pasta - macaroni	30		$1.01 LDS $1.24 ClubCo
Wheat	pasta - other	30		
Fish				
Salmon		8-10		
Tuna		8 - 10		
Vegetables De-hydrated				**Price per can**
Beets		20		
Broccoli		25		$8.78 ClubCo DIY $15.25 BoxMart $23.49 Online
Carrots		25		$8.30 LDS DIY $14.14 BoxMart $17.29 Online
Celery		25		$16.46 ClubCo - D $15.29 Online $12.78 BoxMart

Item	Type	Shelf Life in years	Lbs. per person	Price Comparisons Per pound DIY = self-pack
Corn		25		$9.72 ClubCo - DIY $16.99 Online $13.84 BoxMart
Mushroom		25		$11.98 ClubCo - DIY $17.29 Online
Onion		30		$6.90 LDS DIY $8.44 BoxMart
Peas		25		
Potato	flakes	30		$3.25 (LDS) $8.49 Online
Potato	Shreds	30		$9.25 BoxMart
Potato	Cubes	30		$11.96 $10.39 Online
Sprouts	Seeds	4-5	3	$9.34 BoxMart $12.80 Online
Sweet potatoes		15		$19.89 Online
Tomato	Powder	15		$27.38 BoxMart $28.69 Online

Rotation Pantry

Item	Type	Shelf Life in years	Pounds per person
Baking			
Baking powder		1	
Baking soda		forever	
Brownie Mix		1.5	
Cake Mix		1.5	

Item	Type	Shelf Life in years	Pounds per person
Jell-O		1.5	
Pudding		1	
Jelly, jam		2	
Yeast		2	
Condiments			
BBQ Sauce		1	
Ketchup		1	
Mustard		2	
Salsa		1.5	
Salad dressing		1	
Dairy			
Cheese – Powdered	Parmesan	1	
Fats (total)			**96**
Butter	Canned	2	
Mayonnaise		1	
Peanut butter		2	
Vegetable oil		1	
Fruit			
Drink	Orange	2	
Grains			
Rice	Rice mixes	1	
Tortellini		1	
Meat			
Bacon		1	15
Beef	chunks	1	15
Beef	ground	1	15
Chicken	breasts	2	30
Chili	Canned	2	10
Ham		1	15
Jerky		1	15
Meatballs		1	15

Item	Type	Shelf Life in years	Pounds per person
Pork		1	15
Sausage	patties	1	15
Turkey		1	15
Wieners		1	15
Tuna			10
Salmon			5
Country Ham			5
Spanish Chorizo			5
Dry Salami			5
Seasonings			
Beef Bouillon		2	
Black Pepper		2	
Chicken Bouillon		2	
Garlic Powder		2	
Lemon Juice		**1.5**	
Seasoning salt		5	
Vegetables			
Tomato	canned	1	
Tomato	spaghetti sauce	1	
Olives			
Other			
Pet food		1	

Other Items to Store

Toiletries
- Toothpaste
- Soap
- Shampoo
- Mouthwash
- Deodorant
- Toilet paper
- Razors

Medication
- Aspirin, Tylenol, Aleve, ibuprofen
- Decongestant
- Cough reliever
- Children's Tylenol, cold and flu medication
- Imodium
- Antacids
- Any prescriptions
- Antibiotics

Medical Supplies
- First aid kit
- Gloves
- Masks
- Additional bandages, gauze, tape

Batteries
Store extra batteries for everything you use, and possibly store extra car batteries to store electricity and use for powering things as needed.

Flashlights
Store as many as you can.
Garden Seeds
Store heirloom varieties to insure sustainability.

Lighting
Oil lamps, oil, wicks and candles in case of power outage

Bedding
Extra blankets, pillows and sleeping bags to insure people are warm when fuel is scarce. Extra towels, because laundry may be challenging. Clothesline for drying laundry.

Pet Food
Food for every family member and likely guests.

Sundries
- Laundry Soap
- Bleach for water purification
- Matches
- Fire starters
- Kindling
- Charcoal briquettes
- Extra propane for grills and camp stoves
- Visqueen
- Tarps
- Duct Tape
- Foil

Tip:

Use your electricity-free weekends to learn what to add to your list of items to store.

Also, plan for children to have safe lighting. Some children would be much safer with a flashlight than an oil lamp.

19

Recipes

Breads

Notes: Bread recipes are great stored individually in mylar bags. You'll love the convenience of grabbing a bag to make hot bread to go with your dinner. Plan to give yourself about 4 hours of prep and rising time before you plan to bake your bread. If you are short on time, consider making a quick bread such as corn bread. If you are using a solar oven, allow at least half an hour to the oven to preheat.

Since many bread recipes call for a range of flour to be added, the extra flour is segregated into a baggie. This flour is to be added gradually if needed until the correct texture is achieved. Extra flour (about ¼ cup) is included to sprinkle on the board. You might not need all the flour in the baggie. This is okay.

When you seal your bread recipes in mylar bags, remember to add an oxygen absorber.

Be sure to take the oxygen absorber out before you begin making your bread.

Round French Bread

In a baggie: When making, add:
- 1¼ Cup Flour   1½ Cups water

In the mylar bag: Also needed:
- The baggie   Spray bottle of water
- 2 Cups flour   Cooking spray
- 1 TB. Yeast   Baking sheet
- 2 Tsp. Salt
- 1 oxygen absorber   Time: 4+ hours

Makes: 1 round loaf

Open the bag, discard the oxygen absorber and set aside the baggie. Add the remaining contents to a bowl and add the water. Mix together and let stand for one hour. Measure ¼ Cup of the flour and stir into the dough. Knead the dough on a clean surface adding in as much of the baggie flour as needed to make a smooth elastic dough and knead for about 7 minutes. Cover with a towel and let rise one hour or until doubled. Pat the dough down into a round, let rest 10 minutes, and then shape it into a round, tucking the edges down and around to make a smooth top. Spray a baking sheet with cooking spray, and add the dough. Cover and rise again one hour. Cut a shallow grid pattern in the top and then bake at 425° for 35 minutes, lightly spritzing the top with water halfway through for a chewy crust. Let cool before slicing.

Rustic Sandwich Rolls

Try these with pulled pork or beef with BBQ sauce.

In the baggie:	When making, add:
½ Cup Flour	1¾ Cups water
In the mylar bag:	
The baggie	Also needed:
3 Cups flour	Aluminum foil
2 Tsp. Yeast	Cooking spray
2 Tsp. Salt	Time: 7+ hours or overnight
1 oxygen absorber	Makes: 4 large rolls

Open the bag, discard the oxygen absorber and set aside the baggie. Add the remaining contents to a bowl and add the water. Mix together and let stand for 6 hours or overnight.

Knead the dough on a clean surface adding in as much of the baggie flour as needed. Shape the dough gently into a round, and then cut it into 4 pieces.

Create 4 bread "pans" from a double thickness of foil shaped into "canoes, about 8-9" long and 2" across. Pinching the foil to make the sides stay up. Spray the foil pans with cooking spray, and add the dough pieces, shaping gently to fit. Spray the dough tops lightly with cooking spray and then bake at 450° for 30 minutes, lightly spritzing the top with water halfway through for a chewy crust.

No-Knead Dutch Oven Bread

In the baggie: When making, add:
   ¾ Cup Flour   1½ Cups warm water
In the mylar bag: 2 Tbs. Cornmeal
   The baggie   Also needed:

   3 Cups flour   Dutch Oven
   ¼ Tsp. Yeast   Cooking spray
   1 ½ Tsp. Salt   Rack for cooling
   1 oxygen absorber

Time: 8+ hours or overnight   Makes: 1 loaf

Open the bag, discard the oxygen absorber and set aside the baggie. Add the remaining contents to a bowl and add the water. Mix thoroughly, cover with a towel, and let stand for 8 hours or overnight.

Add ½ Cup of flour from the baggie and stir until very thick. Cover and rise again 2 hours. After an hour place the Dutch oven into the oven and preheat to 450° F.

Carefully remove the Dutch oven from the oven, add cornmeal and the bread dough. Cover and put the Dutch oven back in the oven. Bake 25 minutes, and remove the lid. Bake another 15 – 20 minutes, and remove. Remove the bread to a rack to cool.

No-Knead Artisan Bread

In the baggie:
  2 ¾ Cup Flour
In the mylar bag:
  The baggie
  3 Cups flour
  1 ½ Tsp. Yeast
  1 TB. Salt
  1 TB. Milk powder
Time: overnight

When making, add:
  1¾ + ½ Cups warm water
Also needed:
  Spray bottle with water
  Plastic wrap
  Cooking spray
  Baking sheet

Makes: 2 round loaves

Open the bag, discard the oxygen absorber and set aside the baggie. Add the remaining contents to a bowl and add 1 ¾ cups of water. Mix thoroughly, cover with a plastic wrap, and let stand for 8 - 18 hours or overnight.

Add 1 cup of flour from the baggie and ½ cup of water and stir. Add ½ cup flour and stir in. Sprinkle another ½ flour on the dough and your work surface, remove and knead well (dough will be shaggy). Cover and rise again 90 minutes.

Heat the oven to 450° F. Divide the dough in half and form into two smooth rounds. Spray the baking sheet with cooking spray, add loaves, cut a cross hatch in the tops and mist with water. Bake 30 – 35 minutes, misting with water two or three times periodically before the last 10 minutes. Let cool before slicing.

Focaccia Bread

In the baggie:
  ¾ Cups Flour

In the mylar bag:
  The baggie
  3 Cups flour
  1 Tsp. Yeast
  2 Tsp. Salt
  1 Tb. Italian seasoning - optional
  1 oxygen absorber

When making, add:
  1 ½ Cups water
  ½ Cup Parmesan cheese
  ⅓ Cup olive oil
  ¼ tsp. coarse sea salt

Also needed:
  Cast iron pan
  Cooking spray

Time: 9+ hours or overnight
Makes 2 loaves

Open the bag, discard the oxygen absorber and set aside the baggie. Add the remaining contents to a bowl and add 1 ½ cups water, ¼ cup of Parmesan and 2 Tb. olive oil. Mix together.

From the baggie, spread flour onto the board. Knead the dough on a clean adding in as much of the remaining baggie flour as needed to make a smooth elastic dough and knead for about 5 minutes. Shape into a ball, cover and let rise for 2 hours.

Cut the dough in half. Working with one half at a time, spray a cast iron pan with cooking spray, and add the dough. Pat down and sprinkle with a Tb. of oil, 1 Tb. Parmesan and a sprinkling of salt. Let rest for 30 minutes. Preheat oven to 475 (or use a hot grill). Bake for 20 minutes or until golden. Remove to a rack to cool and repeat with the remaining half of the dough.

Ciabatta Bread

In the baggie:
  2 ½ Cups Flour
In the mylar bag:
  The baggie
  2 Cups flour
  1 ½ Tsp. Yeast
  1 ½ Tsp. Salt
  1 oxygen absorber
Time: 9+ hours or overnight

When making, add:
  1 ¾ Cups water
  2 Tb. Cornmeal
Also needed:
  Plastic wrap
  Spray bottle of water
  Cooking spray
  Baking sheet

Open the bag, discard the oxygen absorber and set aside the baggie. Add the remaining contents to a bowl and add 1 ¼ cups water. Mix together, cover with plastic wrap and let stand for 6 hours or overnight.

Measure ½ cup water and stir carefully into the dough. From the baggie, add a 1 ½ cups of flour, **½ cup at a time**, scraping the sides as you go. Cover with a towel and let rise two hours or until doubled. Knead the dough on a clean surface adding in as much of the remaining baggie flour as needed to make a smooth elastic dough and knead for about 5 minutes.

Pat the dough down into a round, let rest 10 minutes, and then shape it into an oblong, stretching the dough. Spray a baking sheet with cooking spray, and add the dough. Cut a shallow grid pattern in the top and then bake at 450° for 20 - 25 minutes, lightly spritzing the top with water 3 or 4 times for a chewy crust. Makes 1 loaf.

Pizza Crust

1 1/4 cups warm water (100 degrees)
3 Tb. sugar
1 Tb. yeast
1 egg
1 Tb. oil
3 cups of flour, more or less
1 1/2 Tsp. salt

For Pizza: spaghetti sauce, mozzarella cheese (dry, rehydrated) and toppings – pepperoni stick, sliced, sliced olives, etc.

Combine water, sugar and yeast until yeast foams. Stir in lightly beaten egg. In a large bowl, add flour and salt. Whisk to combine. Stir in liquid mixture until a dough forms. Turn out onto a floured board and knead about 50 times until dough is smooth and elastic. Place in a lightly oiled bowl in a warm place and let rise until double, about 1 hour. Preheat oven or grill to 450. Divide dough into 4 pieces, spread with sauce, cheese and toppings and bake until golden.

Flour Tortillas

2 Cups flour
1 tsp. salt
¼ tsp. baking powder
¼ Cup oil
2/3 Cup water

Combine all ingredients and mix well into a ball of dough. Divide dough into 8 pieces. Sprinkle the board with flour and roll out to 1/8th inch thickness. Cook one at a time in a hot skillet for about a minute on each side or until lightly brown in spots.

Fill with taco fillings and eat.

Corn Tortillas
Makes about 15 5" tortillas

1 3/4 cups masa harina
1 1/8 cups water

In a medium bowl, mix together masa harina and hot water until thoroughly combined. Turn dough onto a clean surface and knead until pliable and smooth. If dough is too sticky, add more masa harina; if it begins to dry out, sprinkle with water. Cover dough tightly with plastic wrap and allow to stand for 30 minutes.

Preheat a cast iron skillet or griddle to medium-high.

Divide dough into 15 equal-size balls. Using a tortilla press, a rolling pin, or your hands, press each ball of dough flat between two sheets of plastic wrap.

Immediately place tortilla in preheated pan and allow to cook for approximately 30 seconds, or until browned and slightly puffy. Turn tortilla over to brown on second side for approximately 30 seconds more, then transfer to a plate. Repeat process with each ball of dough. Keep tortillas covered with a towel to stay warm until ready to serve.

Naan Bread

½ Tb (1 package) active dry yeast
1 cup warm water
1/4 cup white sugar
3 tablespoons milk
1 egg, beaten
2 teaspoons salt
4 1/2 cups bread flour
1/4 cup butter, melted

In a large bowl, dissolve yeast in warm water. Let stand about 10 minutes, until frothy. Stir in sugar, milk, egg, salt, and enough flour to make a soft dough. Knead for 6 to 8 minutes on a lightly floured surface, or until smooth. Place dough in an oiled bowl, cover with a damp cloth, and set aside 1 hour, or until the dough has doubled in volume.

Punch down dough,, knead lightly and pinch off small handfuls of dough about the size of a golf ball. Roll into balls, cover and let rest, about 30 minutes.

Meanwhile, preheat a grill, grill pan or griddle until hot.

One by one, roll dough balls into a flat circle, lightly oil pan or grill, and cook for 2 to 3 minutes, or until puffy and lightly browned. Brush uncooked side with butter, and turn over. Brush cooked side with butter, and cook until browned, another 2 to 4 minutes. Remove from grill, and repeat until all the naan has been prepared.

Drop Biscuits

2 cups all-purpose flour
2 tablespoons sugar
4 teaspoons baking powder
1/2 teaspoon cream of tartar
1/2 teaspoon salt
1/2 cup shortening
2/3 cup milk, or reconstituted dry milk
1 egg or equivalent reconstituted dry egg

In a bowl, whisk together flour, sugar, salt, cream of tartar and salt. Cut in shortening until the mixture resembles coarse crumbs. In a bowl, whisk milk and egg. Stir into crumb mixture just until moistened. Drop by heaping spoonfuls 2 in. apart onto an ungreased baking sheet. Bake at 450 degrees F for 10-12 minutes or until golden brown. Serve warm.

Cornbread
Serves 6

2 Cups Cornmeal
2 Tbs. Sugar
1 Tb. Flour
1 Tb. Baking powder
1 ½ Tsp. Salt
2 Cup Buttermilk, or dry milk or buttermilk, reconstituted
3 Eggs, or dry egg equivalent, reconstituted, beaten
4 Tb. Butter, melted

Preheat oven to 450°, and spray a 9X13 baking dish with cooking spray. Combine all ingredients, pour into dish and bake 18 to 20 minutes, until edges pull away from the pan.

Cornmeal Cheddar Scones
Serves 4

¼ Cup Butter or butter flavor crisco
½ Cup Milk, or dry milk, reconstituted
2 Tbs. Brown sugar
½ Cup Cornmeal
1 ½ Cup Flour
¼ Tsp. Salt
1 Tsp. Baking powder
¼ Cup Cheddar cheese, grated, or Parmesan

Preheat the oven to 350. Heat the butter to melt. In a mixing bowl, combine cornmeal, flour, salt and baking powder. Stir to mix well. Stir in brown sugar, and then add cheese and mix through. Add milk and butter and stir until just combined.

Turn out onto a floured surface and form into an 8 inch circle, about ½" thick. Cut the circle into 8 wedges, place on a lightly greased baking sheet and bake 15 to 20 minutes until puffed and golden.

Olive Oil Crackers

1 ½ Cups hard red wheat flour
1 ½ Cups white whole wheat flour (or all-purpose flour)
1 tsp. fine-grain sea salt or table salt
1 cup warm water
⅓ Cup olive oil

special equipment: pasta machine (optional)

Whisk together the flours and salt. Add the water and olive oil. Knead on a floured counter-top.

When you are done mixing, shape the dough into a large ball. Now cut into twelve equal-sized pieces. Gently rub each piece with a bit of olive oil, shape into a small ball and place on a plate. Cover with a clean dishtowel or plastic wrap and let rest at room temperature for 30 - 60 minutes.

Preheat oven to 450F degrees. Insert a pizza stone if you have one.

When the dough is done resting, flatten one dough ball. Using a rolling pin or a pasta machine, shape into a flat strip of dough - Pull the dough out a bit thinner by hand. Set on a floured baking sheet, poke each cracker with a fork to prevent puffing, add any extra toppings, and slide into the oven. Repeat the process for the remaining dough balls, baking in small batches. Bake until deeply golden, and let cool before eating.

Eggs and Cheese

Sun Dried Tomato Scramble
Serves 4

12 Eggs, or dry egg equivalent, reconstituted
⅓ Cup Sun dried tomatoes in oil, chopped or dried, reconstituted
⅓ Cup Chopped green olives
⅓ Cup Feta, crumbled or Parmesan
Pepper, to taste

Scramble egg in greased skillet until almost done. Add tomatoes and olives; heat to serving temperature. Place on serving plates and garnish with cheese.

French Toast Casserole
Serves 6

8 slices stale bread, crusts removed, cut into cubes
2 Cups dry apples, rehydrated
6 Eggs, or dry egg equivalent, reconstituted
1 Cup milk, or dry milk reconstituted
1 ½ tsp. Cinnamon
1 tsp. Vanilla extract
3 Tb. Powdered sugar
Maple syrup (or blueberry, or boysenberry or …)

Preheat oven to 350°. Rehydrate the apples. In a 8" baking dish, add bread cubes, and top with apples. Mix together eggs, milk, vanilla and cinnamon, and pour over apples and bread. Bake about 35 minutes or until set. Sprinkle with powdered sugar and serve.

Ham and Egg Stove Top Pie

Serves 4

1 Cup Ham
2 Tsp. Olive oil
¼ Tsp. Granulated garlic
1 Tsp. Minced dried onion
¼ Tsp. Salt
Water according to couscous package directions
1 Cup Couscous
4 Eggs, or dry egg equivalent, reconstituted
½ Cup Milk, or dry milk, reconstituted
½ Tsp. Oregano, dried
¼ Tsp. Salt
¼ Tsp. Pepper
Dash Tabasco sauce
½ Cup Sharp cheddar cheese, grated, or dried cheese, reconstituted or Parmesan

Beat Eggs, milk, ¼ Tsp. of salt, oregano, pepper, and Tabasco and set aside. Heat oil in a skillet over med high heat. Cook onion and garlic 30 seconds. Add water and remaining salt and bring to a boil. Add couscous. Remove from heat, cover and let sit 5 minutes. Stir in ham. Return to med high heat. Push couscous aside and cook egg mix in skillet for 30 seconds. Stir Eggs, or dry egg equivalent, reconstituted in, and then flatten with a spoon. Sprinkle cheese over top. Cover and cook over low heat about 5 minutes until cheese is melted. Serve hot or at room temperature.

Crepes
Serves 4

6 Eggs, or dry egg equivalent, reconstituted
3 Cups Milk, or dry milk, reconstituted
1 ½ Tsp. Salt
1 ½ Cup Flour
1 ½ Tb. Sugar
3 Tb. Butter, melted

Mix all together with a fork or a mixer until fairly smooth. Ideally, let rest an hour, or overnight, refrigerated. Pour ¼ cup batter onto hot, greased sauté pan and rotate the pan to distribute the batter. When crepe allows, flip and cook second side briefly.

Serve with favorite fillings – jam, Nutella and strawberries, apples and cinnamon, etc.

Straciatella
Serves 8

2 quarts Chicken Stock
4 eggs, or equivalent dry, reconstituted
¼ Cup grated Parmesan Cheese
1 Tb dry Parsley

In a large pot over medium high heat, bring the stock to a simmer. Whish together eggs and cheese. While stirring the stock with a for in a circle in the pot, pour in the eggs in a steady stream, stirring the whole time to form ribbons of the egg in the soup. Stir in parsley, let set 1 minute and serve.

Greek Scramble
Serves 4

8 Eggs, or dry egg equivalent, reconstituted
1 Tb. Parsley, flat leaf, chopped, or ½ Tb. dried
1 Tsp. Oregano, fresh, chopped, or ½ Tsp. dried
2 Tbs. Scallion, minced, or 1 Tsp. minced onion
1 Tb. Olive oil
2 Cups Spinach, chopped, or 1 pkg. frozen, drained or dry, reconstituted
1 Cup Feta, crumbled or Parmesan
1 Cup Tomatoes, diced, canned
Pepper, fresh ground, to taste

Whisk Eggs. Add parsley, oregano, scallion, and pepper.

Heat olive oil in skillet over med high heat. Sauté spinach until wilted and heated through, about 2 - 4 minutes.

Pour eggs over spinach. Pull egg away from edges of pan to allow liquid to flow to bottom.

When Eggs are mostly set, add cheese. Scramble slowly; add tomatoes. Cook until eggs are done and tomatoes are warm.

Southern Grits Soufflé

Serves 4

½ Cup Hominy Grits, not instant
2 ½ Cup Water
½ Tsp. Salt
4 Tb. Butter, from canned or alternate
⅓ Cup Cheddar cheese, grated or Parmesan
Cayenne pepper, ground
3 Eggs, separated or dry egg whites and yolks

In a saucepan over high heat, boil water. Add grits and salt. Cook about 20 minutes, stirring often and remove from heat. Preheat oven to 375°. Butter a 1 quart soufflé dish.

Stir butter, cheese and cayenne into grits. Fold in beaten egg yolks. Beat whites until stiff peaks and fold in. Pour into soufflé dish and bake 35 minutes until golden and firm.

Dutch Babies

Serves 4

4 Eggs, or dry egg equivalent, reconstituted
1 Cup Milk, or dry milk, reconstituted
1 Cup Flour
2 Tbs. Butter
Powdered sugar and applesauce or jam to serve

Preheat oven to 400°. Melt butter in oven in ovenproof skillet (cast iron is my favorite). Mix batter with mixer until no lumps exist. Pour batter into hot pan. Bake for 20 minutes and serve.

Cheese Soufflé

Serves 2

4 Eggs, separated or dry egg equivalent, reconstituted whites and yokes
1 Cup Cheddar cheese, grated or dehydrated cheese, rehydrated or Parmesan
4 Tb. Butter
4 Tb. Flour
1 Cup Milk, or dry milk, reconstituted
½ Tsp. Salt
Dash Cayenne pepper, ground

Preheat oven to 350°. Butter a 1 quart soufflé dish or other dish with tall sides.

In a saucepan over medium high heat, sauté flour and butter for 3 minutes. Whisk in milk raise heat and stir until thickened. Remove from heat, add cheese, seasonings and egg yolk, stirring to combine.

In a separate bowl, beat egg whites to stiff peaks and fold gently into cheese mixture. Pour into dish and bake 35 minutes. Serve immediately.

Huevos Rancheros (Mexican Style Eggs)
Serves 4

1 Can Diced tomatoes, Mexican style
2 Cups Diced potatoes with onion, like Simply Potato, or dehydrated potatoes and onion, rehydrated
½ Cup Vegetable broth or equivalent bouillon
1 Tb. Tomato paste or tomato powder and water
1 Tsp. Chili powder
½ Tsp. Cumin, ground
¼ Tsp. Salt
⅛ Tsp. Black pepper
4 Eggs, or powder egg equivalent, reconstituted
½ Cup Cheddar cheese, grated, or dry cheese, rehydrated or Parmesan
4 Tsp. Cilantro, optional

In a large skillet, combine first 8 ingredients; stir gently. Bring to a boil and cover; reduce heat, and simmer for 5 minutes.

Scramble eggs in a small bowl, and pour on top of potato mixture. Cover and simmer for 5 minutes or until eggs are done. Sprinkle cheese over eggs and cover until cheese melts about 20 seconds. Portion out skillet onto four plates, and sprinkle with cilantro.

Cheddar Cheese Soup
Serves 4

1 ½ Cup Cheddar cheese, grated, rehydrated
1 Can Stock 12.5 Oz., Chicken or beef
2 Tbs. Butter
3 Tb. Flour
⅓ Cup Onion, grated, or 1 Tb. dry rehydrated
1 ½ Cup Milk, or dry milk, reconstituted
¼ Tsp. Cayenne pepper, ground

In a saucepan, melt butter and sauté flour 2 minutes. Whisk in onion, stock and cook 2 minutes. Add milk and cayenne. Stir until thickened. Stir in cheese until melted and serve.

Cheese Strata
Serves 4

4 Bread slices
½ Cup Cheddar cheese, grated, or dry cheese, rehydrated or Parmesan
2 Tsp. Mustard
2 Eggs, or dry egg equivalent, reconstituted, beaten
1 Cup Milk, or dry milk, reconstituted
Salt and pepper, to taste

Preheat oven to 375. Spread mustard on half the bread slices and form into sandwiches with cheese and another slice of bread. Place them side by side in a loaf pan. Beat together eggs, milk and pour over sandwiches. Bake until browned and set about 30 minutes.

Chili Relleno Casserole

Serves 4

3 Cans Diced green chilies, 4 Oz.
4 Corn tortillas, cut in strips
1 lb. Cheddar cheese, grated, or dry cheese, rehydrated or Parmesan
½ Cup Salsa
8 Eggs, or dry egg equivalent, reconstituted
½ Cup Milk, or dry milk, reconstituted
1 Tsp. Salt

Preheat oven to 375.

Layer chilies in the bottom of a greased 9 inch square baking dish. Top with half of the tortilla strips, and half the cheese and all of the salsa. Repeat the first 3 layers.

Beat together eggs, milk, salt, and pour over casserole.

Bake for 35 to 40 minutes.

Tip:

Many families plan to make fuel stretch by running a generator 4 hours a day. This could be enough to keep your refrigerator cool and possibly be enough time to heat water, shower and do laundry. Clean is also good for morale.

Beans

White Bean Enchiladas with Salsa Verde
Serves 4 - 6

2 Tbs. Olive oil
1 Tb. Garlic, minced
2 Cans Cannellini beans, 15.5 Oz., drained, or dried and soaked overnight
⅓ Cup Chicken stock
1 dozen Corn tortillas
2 Cup Salsa verde
2 Cup Jack cheese, grated, or dry cheese, rehydrated
Cooking spray

Preheat oven to 350. In a sauce pan, heat oil, and sauté garlic. Add beans and chicken stock. Simmer beans 5 to 7 minutes until soft, then mash the beans. Remove from heat.

Spray a baking dish with cooking spray. Coat tortillas on both sides with cooking spray, and heat one at a time in a skillet until pliable. Roll about ¼ Cup of bean mixture in each tortilla, and place seam side down in the dish.

Top with salsa and cheese; bake until bubbly, about 20 minutes.

Chickpea and Tomato Stew
Serves 6

2 Tbs. Olive oil
½ Cup Shallots, minced, or ¼ Cup minced onion
2 Tsp. Curry powder
1 Tsp. Cumin, ground
1 Can Chickpeas, 15 Oz.
1 Can Diced Tomatoes,14.5 Oz.
1 Cup Tomato sauce or spaghetti sauce
Sour cream, or reconstituted sour cream powder, for serving

Heat the oil in a large skillet over medium high heat and sauté the shallots (or onion) until sizzling, 5 minutes. Add curry powder and cumin and cook another minute. Add chickpeas, tomatoes and sauce and simmer 10 minutes.

Tuscan White Bean Soup
Serves 8

2 ¼ Cups Cannellini beans
12 Cups water
1 Tb. Garlic salt
2 tp. Onion powder
2 strips bacon, optional
¼ Cup Olive oil
1 tsp. dry Rosemary, crumbled

Add beans, water, garlic salt, onion powder and bacon to the pot, cover and simmer one hour. Remove bacon, turn heat to low, stir in olive oil and rosemary, and gently cook until beans are done, about 15 to 20 minutes.

Pasta e Fagioli Soup
Serves 8

2 Tb Cup olive oil
3 strips bacon, diced, optional
⅓ Cup dry diced Onion
½ Cup dry Celery
1 Tb. Garlic
1 Tsp. dry oregano
½ tsp. red pepper flakes
2 Cans diced tomatoes, 14.5 oz. each
2 Cans Cannellini beans
4 Cups Chicken stock, or soup base with water
1 tsp. Salt
8 oz. small pasta shapes
2 Tb. dry parsley
Black pepper
1 Cup Parmesan Cheese
2 Tb. Olive oil

In a soup pot, heat the olive oil and cook the bacon. Add vegetables, garlic, oregano, pepper flakes, tomatoes, beans and stock. Cook until vegetables are tender, about 20 minutes. Add salt, and pasta and cook until pasta is tender, about 10 minutes. Stir in parsley, and pepper and serve sprinkled with cheese and drizzled with olive oil.

Orzo and Garbanzo Soup
Serves 4

½ Cup Orzo pasta
¼ Cup Olive oil
½ Onion, chopped, or ¼ Cup dry, rehydrated
2 Tsp. Garlic, minced
½ Tsp. Rosemary, dried
½ Tsp. Sage, dried rubbed
1 Can Diced tomatoes with liquid, 14.5 Oz.
3 Cups Broth
1 Can Garbanzo beans 14 Oz., drained
¼ Cup Parsley, flat leaf, chopped or 2 Tbs. dried
¼ Cup Parmesan cheese, grated

Heat oil in a skillet over medium heat. Add onion and sauté 4 minutes. Add garlic, rosemary and sage cooking 1 minute more. Add tomatoes and cook 10 minutes. Add broth and beans cooking 5 minutes more.

Puree in blender (optional). Return to soup pot and heat to a boil. Add orzo and cook until al dente. Season to taste. Garnish with parsley and cheese.

Bacon and Beans Casserole
Serves 4

1 lb. Bacon, cut into 1" pieces
1 lb. white beans, soaked overnight in water, drained
3 Cups apples – dry, rehydrated
½ C dry onion slices, rehydrated
1 Cup dry potato chunks, rehydrated
Sal and pepper
2 Cups water
1 Tb. parsley, dry

Preheat oven to 325. In an ovenproof pan with lid, cook bacon until crispy – 10 – 15 minutes. Add beans, apples, onion and potatoes. Season to taste. Add water and bake until the beans are done, about 2 hours.

Simple Hummus
Serves 4

2 Cans Garbanzo beans, 14 Oz., ½ Cup liquid reserved
½ Cup Lemon juice
½ Cup Tahini
⅓ Cup Olive oil
3 Garlic cloves, smashed
Salt, to taste

Puree in food processor/blender until smooth. Serve immediately or refrigerate up to 4 days.

This is wonderful served with Olive Oil Crackers.

Essential Bean Salad
Serves 4

4 Cup Mung (or other) beans, precooked
1 Tb. Lemon juice, fresh
4 Tb. Red onion, minced, or 1 Tb. dry onion, rehydrated
¼ Cup Olive oil
½ Cup Parsley, flat leaf, chopped, or 2 Tbs. dried
Salt and pepper, to taste

Combine vinegar, onion, salt, pepper, and olive oil. Add drained beans to mix and toss. Add parsley just before serving and adjust seasonings. May be served at room temperature or refrigerated.

Quinoa and Bean Burritos
Serves 4

1 Cup Quinoa
2 Tsp. Smokey sweet pepper blend seasoning
1 Can Red kidney beans, 15 Oz., drained, slightly mashed
1 ½ Cup Salsa
8 Whole wheat tortillas
1 Cup Mexican cheese blend, shredded r dry cheese reconstituted

Preheat oven to 350°. Spray baking sheet with nonstick cooking spray. Combine quinoa and pepper. Cook quinoa following package directions. Stir in beans and two thirds of the salsa. Heat tortillas in microwave for 45 seconds. Place ½ cup of bean mixtures on each tortilla and fold. Place seam down on baking sheet. Spray burritos with nonstick spray and top with remaining salsa and cheese. Bake 12 minutes and serve.

Crock Pot Southwestern Bean Soup
Serves 6

1 Can Kidney beans, 15 Oz., rinsed and drained
1 Can Black beans, 15 Oz., drained and rinsed
1 Can Mexican style stewed tomatoes, 14.5 Oz.
3 Cups Water
1 pkg. Corn, whole kernel, frozen, or 1 ½ C dried,
1 Cup Carrot, sliced, optional or dried
1 Onion, chopped, or ½ Cup dry onion, rehydrated
1 Can Diced green chilies
2 Tbs. Bouillon
1 ½ Tsp. Chili powder
2 Tsp. Garlic, minced
⅓ Cup Flour
¼ Cup Cornmeal
1 Tsp. Baking powder
Dash of pepper
1 Beaten egg white, or dry egg white reconstituted
2 Tbs. Milk, or dry milk, reconstituted
1 Tb. Oil

Combine in 4 quart crock pot: water, beans, undrained tomatoes, carrot, onion, undrained chili peppers, bouillon, chili powder and garlic. Cook on low for 10 hours or high for 5 hours.

In medium mixing bowl combine flour, cornmeal, baking powder and pepper. In separate bowl combine egg white, Milk, or dry milk, reconstituted and oil. Mix dry and wet ingredients with fork just until combined. Drop dumplings into mounds on top of soup. Cover and cook for 20 30 minutes more until toothpick comes out clean. Serve in individual bowls topped with a dumpling.

Potluck Beans

Serves 6

4 Bacon slices, diced
¼ Cup Onion, chopped, or dry, rehydrated
1 Can Green chilies, diced, 4 Oz.
1 Can Black beans, 15 Oz., drained
1 Can Kidney beans, 15 Oz., rinsed and drained
1 Can Pork and beans, 16 Oz.
1 Can Chili con carne, 16 Oz.
2 Tbs. Ketchup or 2 Tb tomato powder + 1 tsp. water
2 Tbs. Brown sugar
½ Tsp. Garlic powder

Brown diced bacon and onion together in a large Dutch oven; drain off excess fat. Add remaining ingredients; stir well. Simmer 15 to 20 minutes.

Three Bean Chili

Serves 8

2 Cans Kidney or pinto beans, 15 Oz.
2 Cans White or great northern beans, 15 Oz.
1 Can Lima beans, 15 Oz.
1 ½ Cup Salsa

Combine all ingredients and heat to serving temperature.

Toasted Bean Tortilla Sandwich
Serves 2

2 Flour tortillas
⅓ Cup Refried beans, 15 Oz.
1 Tb. Chili sauce
2 Tbs. Cheddar cheese, grated, or dry cheese, rehydrated or Parmesan
1 ½ Tsp. Olive oil
Salsa
Sour cream, or sour cream powder, reconstituted (optional)

Combine beans and chili sauce then layer ingredients in order listed. Place in an oiled frying pan with a weight on top (a plate with a Can on it); cook until crisp. Flip and cook until that side is crisp. Serve with sour cream and salsa.

Tomato and Bean Casserole

Serves 4

3 Can Beans any type 14 ¼
2 Cans Diced Tomatoes, 14.5 Oz. diced
1 Can Diced green chilies, 4 Oz.
1 Onion, chopped, or ½ Cup dry, rehydrated
2 Cup Cheddar cheese, grated, or dry cheese, rehydrated or Parmesan
Salt and pepper, to taste

Preheat oven to 400°. In a bowl, combine beans, chilies and seasonings. In a casserole dish, layer beans, onions, tomatoes and cheese. Repeat with remaining ingredients, ending with cheese. Bake 20 minutes.

Hopping John
Serves 4

1 Can Black eyed peas, 16 Oz.
1 Cup Uncle Bens converted rice
1 ½ Cup Onion, chopped or ½ Cup dry onion, rehydrated
1 ½ Tsp. Garlic salt
½ Tsp. Salt
2 Tsp. Chili powder
1 ½ Cup Cheddar cheese, grated, or Parmesan

Drain black, eyed peas, reserving liquid. Add water to make 2 and a half cups. In a large skillet, combine black, eyed peas, liquid, rice, onions, garlic salt, salt and chili powder. Stir and bring to a boil; cover and simmer 20 minutes. Remove from heat. Sprinkle with cheese. Cover and let stand until liquid is absorbed and cheese melted, about 5 minutes.

Chili Tortilla Bake
Serves 4

2 Cans Chili with beans
1 Onion, chopped, or ½ Cup dry, rehydrated
2 Cup Cheddar cheese, grated, or ½ CupParmesan
6 Flour tortillas, 8 inch

Layer chili, onion and torn tortillas in a baking dish, top with cheese and bake at 350° 20 minutes.

Jiffy Chili and Cornbread
Serves 8

2 Cans Chili with beans
2 Cup Cheddar cheese, grated, or dry cheese, rehydrated or 1 Cup Parmesan
1 package Jiffy corn muffin mix
⅓ Cup Milk, or dry milk, reconstituted
1 Egg, or dry egg equivalent

Preheat oven to 400. In a mixing bowl combine milk, egg and corn muffin mix. In a baking dish layer chili, cheese and top with batter. Bake 25 minutes or until golden.

Red Beans and Rice
Serves 8

1 lb. red kidney beans
8 Cups water
1 pint canned ground beef
1 tsp. garlic
1/3 Cup dry onion
2 Tb. Dried parsley
2 Bay leaves
seasoning salt to taste
1/2 Tsp. Cayenne pepper
2 Cups Rice, cooked in 4 cups water with 2 tsp. salt

In a large pot, cover beans in water and boil for 2 minutes. Turn off heat and let stand, covered, for 1 hour. Drain and rinse beans. Add 8 cups of water, garlic, onion, and bay. Simmer gently for 2 - 4 hours until tender. Stir in seasoning salt and cayenne. Remove bay leaves. Cook rice. To serve, spoon rice into bowls, spoon beans over.

Tip:

When you soak beans, discard the water from the first soaking period and start with fresh water. This will remove most of the cause of the musicality which beans are known to produce in those who eat them.

Grains

Mexican Polenta Pie
Serves 6

3/4 Cup Cornmeal
2 Cup Water
¼ Tsp. Salt
1 Egg, beaten
1 Can Chili beans, 16 Oz., drained
3/4 Cup Pepper jack cheese, grated, or 1/3 Cup Parmesan and 1 tsp. red pepper flakes
⅓ Cup Corn or taco chips, crushed

Preheat oven to 375°. Grease pie plate, 9 x1 ¼ inches, with nonstick cooking spray. Mix cornmeal, water and salt in medium saucepan. Bring to a boil, stirring constantly; reduce heat to medium. Cook about 6 minutes, stirring frequently, until the mixture is very thick. Remove from heat; let stand 5 minutes, stir in egg.

Spread cornmeal mixture in the pie plate and bake uncovered for 15 minutes. Spread beans over cornmeal mixture; sprinkle with cheese and corn chips. Bake uncovered for an additional 20 minutes or until center is set. Let stand 5 minutes before serving.

Minnesota Wild Rice Soup
Serves 8

3 Tb. Butter
1 Cup carrots, diced, rehydrated
1 Cup onion, diced, rehydrated
1 Cup celery, diced, rehydrated
¼ Cup flour
2 quarts chicken broth (8 Cups)
¾ Cup Wild rice
½ tsp. salt
1 Can evaporated milk, 5 oz.
2 Tb dry parsley

Heat the butter in a soup pot and sauté the carrots, onion and celery. Reduce heat to low and add the flour. Cook, stirring 2 minutes. Add the stock and stir well. Add the wild rice and simmer until rice is tender, about 45 minutes. Stir in salt, milk, parsley and serve.

Baked Cheesy Grits
Serves 4

1 quart milk powder, reconstituted (4 cups)
½ cup butter or margarine
1 cup uncooked grits
1 tsp. salt
½ tsp. white pepper
1 cup shredded Cheddar cheese, dry rehydrated
⅓ cup butter
½ cup grated Parmesan cheese

Preheat oven to 350 degrees. Lightly grease a medium baking dish. In a medium saucepan, bring the milk to a boil in a pot over medium heat. Melt 1/2 cup butter in the boiling milk. Gradually mix in the grits, and cook 5 minutes, stirring constantly.

Remove from heat, and season with salt and pepper. Beat with a whisk or electric mixer until smooth. Mix in the cheese and 1/3 cup butter. Transfer to the prepared baking dish, and sprinkle with Parmesan cheese. Bake I hour.

Barley Mushroom Casserole
Serves 4

½ Cup dried mushrooms
½ Cup pearl barley
1 ½ tsp. salt
1 tsp. garlic
2 Tb. minced onion
2 Tb. Butter or lard
¼ Tsp. marjoram
Black pepper

Soak the mushrooms is water 30 minutes, and drain reserving liquid. Add water to mushroom liquid to equal 3 cups. Add mushroom, barley and liquid to an oven and stove proof pot with lid. Stir in salt and simmer until barley is tender, about an hour. Preheat the oven to 350. Add onion, butter, marjoram and pepper, cover and bake 30 minutes.

Baked Polenta
Serves 6

1 Cup dry polent or coarsely ground dry corn
3 1/2 Cups water
1/2 Cup dry corn kernels, rehydrated
1 tsp. Salt
1/2 tsp. black pepper
1/3 Cup grated Parmesan cheese
2 Tb. Butter

Preheat oven to 350 degrees. Oil an 8 x 8 baking dish. In the dish mix polenta, corn, water, salt and pepper. Bake 50 minutes. Stir in cheese and butter and bake 10 minutes more.

Rice, Barley, Lentil and Mushroom Pilaf
Serves 4 - 6

1/2 Cup Brown rice
1/2 Cup Pearl barley
1/2 Cup dried lentils
3 1/3 Cups chicken or vegetable stock
2 tsp dijon mustard
1 Tb. Soy sauce
1 oz. dried mushrooms

In a large sauce pan, combine all ingredients and stir well. Bring to a boil, and then reduce to simmer and cook, covered for about 45 - 55 minutes. Alternately, bake in a preheated oven.

Cheesy Corn Bread
Serves 8

1 ¼ Cup Cornmeal
3/4 Cup Flour
2 ½ Tsp. Baking powder
½ Tsp. Salt
1 Cup Buttermilk, or dry milk or buttermilk, reconstituted
1 Egg, or powdered equivalent
⅓ Cup Extra, sharp cheddar cheese, shredded, or dry reconstituted
¼ Cup Parmesan cheese, grated, or dry cheese, rehydrated
1 Cup Corn, fresh or frozen or dry, rehydrated
1 ½ Tsp. Jalapeño pepper (optional), minced or ¼ tsp red pepper flakes

Preheat the oven to 400°. Spray either a 8 inch pan or 12 muffin tin, with cooking spray or use paper liners for muffins.

In a large bowl, combine the cornmeal, flour, baking powder, salt, cheeses, corn and pepper (if using).

In small bowl, beat together egg and buttermilk. Pour wet mixture over dry. Stir until blended, but do NOT over mix. Transfer to the pan or muffin tin.

Bake for 20 to 25 minutes, until golden brown.

Bulgur and Tomato Salad

Serves 2

1 Cup Bulgur
1 Can Tomatoes, 14.5 Oz., diced
2 Tbs. Olive oil
2 Tsp. Garlic, minced
½ Tsp. Oregano, dried
¼ Tsp. Allspice, ground
1 Can Beef stock
2 Tsp. Anchovy paste, optional
¼ Cup Onion, chopped or 2 Tb. dry, rehydrated

In a skillet over medium heat; Sauté onion and garlic until softened. Add vegetables and spices and simmer 10 minutes. Add broth and bring to a boil. Add bulgur, cover and set heat to low and cook 20 minutes. Remove from heat, let it set 10 minutes and serve.

Baked Rice Pilaf with Carrots
Serves 4

3 Tb. Butter or margarine
½ Cup diced carrots, canned or dry and rehydrated
1 Cup long grain rice, rinsed in water and drained
1 ½ Cups water
1 tsp. salt
½ tsp. pepper

Preheat oven to 350. In a stove and oven safe pot with lid melt butter over medium high heat. Add carrots and rice and stir for two minutes. Add water, salt and pepper. Bring to a simmer and then cover and bake 20 minutes.

Wild Mushroom Risotto with Shrimp and Peas
Serves 8

2 package Wild Mushroom Risotto Mix, 5.45 Oz. each,
1 pint canned shrimp
1 Tb. Olive oil
1 ½ Cup Peas, frozen

Remove peas and shrimp from freezer. In a microwavable bowl, prepare both boxes of risotto according to directions on box. In a large skillet, heat shrimp in oil until heated through, about 3 minutes. When shrimp are cooked, remove from heat, and add peas to skillet; sauté them for about 2 minutes.

When risotto is done and broth is absorbed, toss with peas and shrimp.

Ham

Grilled Cheese With Apple And Ham
Serves 4

1 Apples, chopped, or 1 Cup dried apples rehydrated and chopped
¼ Cup Mayonnaise
⅓ Cup Walnuts, chopped and toasted
4 Cheddar cheese, slices, or dry grated cheese, rehydrated
8 Bread slices
4 Ham slices
4 Tb. Butter

Combine apple, walnuts and mayonnaise in a small bowl. Top 4 slices of bread with a slice of ham, ¼ of the cheese, and ¼th of the apple mixture. Top with a 2nd slice of bread, butter the outsides and grill in a skillet over medium high on each side until golden.

Ham and Rice Casserole
Serves 6

1 package Rice A Roni, any flavor
1 Cup Ham, diced
1 Can Cream of chicken soup
1 Can Cream of mushroom soup
1 Can Peas, or other vegetable

Prepare Rice A Roni according to package directions. Stir in other ingredients and cook 10 minutes over medium high until hot and bubbling.

Twice Baked Potatoes with Ham
Serves 4

4 Potatoes, russet, or 4 Cups dry potato slices or dices, reconstituted
1 ½ Cup Ham, diced
2 Cup Cheddar cheese, grated, or dry cheese, rehydrated or Parmesan
¼ Cup Butter
Salt and pepper, to taste

Preheat oven to 400°.

If using whole potatoes:

>Bake potatoes until just done.
>Slice open tops, and scoop out potato leaving a ¼ inch shell.
>
>Mix potatoes with remaining ingredients, then return to shell, and reheat. Note: You can cook the potatoes the night before if that works better.

With dry potatoes:

>In a baking dish, layer potatoes, and sprinkle in ham. Drizzle with melted butter and stir. Season with salt and pepper, sprinkle with cheese and bake until hot and golden.

Ham and Asian Noodles
Serves 4

2 Cup Water
1 package Broccoli carrots and water chestnut, frozen 16 Oz. or 1 C each dried carrots, celery and broccoli rehydrated
2 package Oriental flavor instant ramen noodles, with seasoning packets
¼ Tsp. Ginger, ground
1 Ham steak, or 1 pint canned ham
2 Tbs. Green onions, chopped or 1 Tb. minced onion, soaked in water

In a large nonstick skillet, combine 2 cups water, frozen vegetables, noodles, broken into pieces, ginger and seasoning packets; bring to a boil.

While coming to a boil, dice ham into bite sized pieces. Reduce heat; cover and simmer 3 minutes, or until noodles are done, stirring occasionally.

Add ham to skillet and heat. Stir in onions and serve.

Ham and Broccoli Casserole

Serves 4

2 Cups dry broccoli
4 Tb. Butter, margarine or shortening
¼ Cup Flour
1 Tb. Dijon mustard
2 Cups milk, from powder, reconstituted
1 Tsp. Dried sage
Salt and pepper to taste
1 pint canned ham, diced
½ Cup Bread crumbs
¼ Cup Parmesan cheese, grated
Cooking spray

Preheat the oven to 350.

Spray a large baking dish with cooking spray.

Heat the broccoli in hot water until tender, and drain. Layer the broccoli in the prepared dish and season with salt and pepper.

Melt butter and flour together in a saucepan and cook 2 minutes. Add milk, mustard and sage, and cook, stirring, until thickened, about 12 minutes. Season with salt and pepper. Sprinkle ham on top of the broccoli. Pour the sauce over the broccoli and ham. Top with bread crumbs and Parmesan cheese and bake for 35 minutes or until golden and bubbly.

Ham and Noodles Casserole
Serves 6

8 oz. Egg noodles
4 Tb. Butter or margarine
1 C dry onion, rehydrated
2 eggs, or equivalent powdered egg, reconstituted
1 small can evaporated milk, 5 oz.
1 pint home canned ham, diced
¼ tsp. pepper
1 tsp. paprika

Preheat oven to 350. Cook noodles in salted boiling water according to package directions. Drain and return to pot. Add butter and onions to hot noodles and stir to combine. Add ham and stir together. In a bowl, beat together eggs and evaporated milk. Layer noodles in the bottom of a baking dish. Pour egg mixture over top and sprinkle with paprika. Bake 40 minutes or until set.

Baked Ham Risotto
Serves 6

2 Cups Arborio or Carnaroli Rice
5 Cups chicken or vegetable stock or soup base and water
4 Tb. Butter
1 Tb oil
1 pint home canned ham, diced
¾ Cup Parmesan cheese
Salt and Pepper to taste
1 Tb. dry parsley

Preheat oven to 400. Place rice, stock and butter in an ovenproof dish, cover with foil and bake 30 minutes. Meanwhile sauté ham in oil until slightly brown. Stir ham, cheese, salt, pepper and parsley for about 2 minutes to thicken it.

Note: Any leftover risotto can be formed into patties or balls, rolled in breadcrumbs mixed with Parmesan, and fried. Delicious!

Baked Ham Carbonara
Serves 6

1 lb. Spaghetti, ziti or fettuccine
1 Tb. Oil
1 pint home canned ham, diced
6 Eggs, or equivalent dry egg, reconstituted
1 Can Evaporated Milk, 12 oz.
2 Cups Milk or dry milk and water equivalent
½ Cup grated Parmesan cheese

Preheat oven to 350. Cook spaghetti I boiling salted water until tender, drain, then layer in a baking dish. In a skillet, brown ham in oil. Spread ham over pasta in the baking dish. In a bowl, whisk together evaporated milk, milk eggs, and Parmesan cheese. Pour over ham and pasta, and bake 30 minutes or until set.

Crispy Ham and Rice Omelet
Serves 4

1 ½ Cups cooked rice (½ Cup raw, cooked w/ 1 Cup water)
2 Tb. Oil
1 pint home canned ham, diced
2 Tb. dry Onion, rehydrated, minced
1 Tsp. Red pepper flakes
¾ Cup dry Peas, rehydrated or other vegetable, chopped
6 eggs, beaten or equivalent egg product, rehydrated

Preheat oven to 350. In a skillet heat the oil, and brown the ham, then add onions, pepper, peas, and eggs, and stir in. Book without stirring 5 minutes and then bake 5 minutes or until set.

Creamy Ham and Potato Soup
Serves 6

3 cups dry potato cubes
1/4 cup dry diced celery
1/4 cup dry diced onion
1/4 Cup dry diced carrot
1 cup diced cooked ham
1 Quart chicken stock (4 cups) or soup base
1/2 tsp. salt
1 tsp. pepper
5 TB. butter, margarine or shortening
5 TB. all-purpose flour
2 cups milk or reconstituted dry milk

Add the vegetables, ham, stock, salt and pepper to a soup pot and simmer gently for 30 - 45 minutes. Meanwhile, in a separate saucepan, cook butter and flour, stirring for 3 minutes. Whisk in milk and cook until thickened, stirring constantly. Add milk mixture to the soup pot and serve. (May be garnished with grated cheese or crumbled bacon if desired.)

Seafood, Shrimp

Baked Creole Shrimp
Serves 2

2 Tbs. Worcestershire sauce
2 Tbs. Butter, melted
2 Tsp. Creole seasoning
2 Tsp. Olive oil
Cooking spray, olive oil flavored
1 lb. Shrimp, peeled, frozen or 1 pint canned

Preheat oven to 450°. Combine first 4 ingredients in a small bowl. Put shrimp in a 11 X 7 baking dish that has been sprayed with cooking spray. Pour butter mixture over the shrimp, stirring to coat. Bake at 450 for 8 minutes, or until shrimp are heated through.

Mediterranean Shrimp with Couscous
Serves 4

1 lb. Shrimp, medium, peeled and deveined or 1 pint canned shrimp
1 Can Tomatoes, 14.5 Oz. diced, Italian style
3/4 Cup Water
1 package Couscous mix with toasted pine nuts
½ Cup Golden raisins
½ Cup Feta cheese, crumbled or Parmesan

Rinse shrimp and pat dry. In a large skillet over medium high heat combine tomatoes, seasoning packet from couscous and bring to a boil. Add shrimp and cook 2 or 3 minutes until shrimp is opaque. Add couscous and raisons, cover and remove from heat. Let stand 5 minutes, stir in feta and serve.

Spiced Garlic Shrimp
Serves 4

1 ½ lb. Shrimp, large, peeled and deveined or 1 pint canned shrimp
½ Cup Olive oil
3 Tsp. Garlic, minced
1 ½ Tsp. Paprika
1 Tsp. Cumin, ground
Salt and pepper, to taste

Preheat the broiler. In a large oven proof skillet on the stove over medium heat, heat oil and garlic until golden. Add shrimp and spices and stir to coat. Broil 5 to 10 minutes until shrimp are done and the oil is bubbly.

Shrimp with Rosemary Cannellini Beans
Serves 4

1 lb. Shrimp or 1 pint canned shrimp
1 Tb. Olive oil, plus more for serving
1 Tsp. Garlic, minced
2 Tbs. Parsley, flat leaf, chopped, or 1 Tb. dried
2 Tsp. Rosemary or sage, chopped or 1 Tsp. dried
2 Cup Cannellini beans, cooked or canned
½ Cup Broth – chicken or vegetable, or bouillon with water
Salt and pepper, to taste

Heat olive oil over medium heat in frying pan. Add garlic, parsley and rosemary; cook 1 minute. Add shrimp, beans and seasonings; cook 1 minute. Add broth, simmering 2 minutes more until shrimp are pink. Season to taste. Drizzle shrimp and beans with olive oil; sprinkle with parsley and serve.

Garlic Shrimp
Serves 4

2 lb. Shrimp, or 2 pints canned shrimp
¼ Cup Parsley, fresh, chopped
⅓ Cup Olive oil
4 Garlic, large cloves, thinly slivered or 4tsp. garlic
Salt and pepper, to taste

In a large skillet, combine oil and garlic over medium heat.

Cook until garlic sizzles. Add cumin and paprika. Stir, and raise the heat to medium high. Add shrimp, salt, and pepper. Cook until shrimp are just pink and heated through, stirring occasionally.

Shrimp in Lime Juice
Serves 4

1 ½ lb. Shrimp, medium, peeled and deveined, or 1 pint canned shrimp
½ Cup Lime juice
¼ Cup Sugar
1 Tb. Nam pla (fish sauce)
2 Tbs. Corn oil
1 Tsp. Garlic, minced
½ Tsp. Red pepper flakes
Cilantro, chopped, optional

Combine lime juice, sugar, and nam pla. Place oil in a large skillet over high heat. After one minute, add garlic and pepper flakes. Cook until garlic starts to brown. Add lemon juice mixture, and cook until it's reduced by about half, 3 to 5 minutes. There will only be about ¼ cup of liquid in the skillet. Add shrimp, and cook over high heat. Shrimp will begin to turn pink immediately. Stir after 2 minutes of cooking. Continue cooking until shrimp are completely pink, about 2 minutes longer. Taste, and adjust seasoning if necessary. Garnish with cilantro and serve.

Shrimp Salad Melts
Serves 4

1 ¼ lb. Bay shrimp or 2 cans tiny shrimp
¼ Cup Mayonnaise
½ Tsp. Dill, dried
2/3 Cups Mozzarella cheese grated, or 1/3 Cup Parmesan
Salt and pepper, to taste
1 Loaf of focaccia, ciabatta or other wide soft bread

Preheat the broiler, oven or toaster oven. Halve the bread horizontally. Mix together shrimp, dill and mayonnaise. Spread the bottom of the bread with the shrimp mixture and more mayonnaise if desired. Top with cheese and place under the broiler and heat until both halves until bubbly. Put the top half back on, slice and serve.

Lemon Garlic Quick Baked Shrimp
Serves 4

1 lb. Shrimp, peeled and deveined, or 1 pint canned shrimp
3 Tb. Lemon juice
¼ Cup Olive oil
3 Tsp. Garlic, minced
Salt and pepper, to taste
½ Cup Parmesan cheese, grated
2/3 Cups Bread crumbs

Preheat the oven to 400°. Line a rimmed baking sheet with foil.
In a bowl, whisk together olive oil, lemon juice, and garlic.
Add the shrimp, and toss to coat. Season generously with salt and pepper. Add Parmesan and breadcrumbs, tossing to coat. Spread shrimp on the baking sheet, and bake 5 minutes, or until golden and just cooked through.

Shrimp in BBQ Sauce
Serves 4

2 lb. Shrimp, medium, peeled and deveined, or 2 pints canned shrimp
4 Tb. Butter, unsalted
2 Tbs. Worcestershire sauce
1 Lemon, juiced
Salt and pepper, to taste

Over high heat, melt butter in a large skillet. When it is melted, add shrimp and Worcestershire sauce. Cook until the sauce is glossy and thick, stirring occasionally, about 5 minutes. If the sauce becomes too dry, add a tablespoon or two of water. When the shrimp are heated through, salt and pepper to taste. Stir in lemon juice. Serve over bread or rice.

Crab and Shrimp Melts
Serves 4

1 Can Crab
1 Can Bay shrimp
4 English muffins split
⅓ Cup Mayonnaise
2 Tbs. Lemon juice
2 Tbs. Onion, grated, or 1 Tb. dry, rehydrated
½ Cup Cheddar cheese, grated, or dry cheese, rehydrated or Parmesan

Toast bread or English muffins and preheat broiler. Combine crab, shrimp, mayonnaise, lemon, onion and cheese. Top bread with mixture and broil until cheese is bubbly.

Seafood, Tuna

Tuna Melts
Serves 2

2 Cans Tuna
3 Tb. Mayonnaise
2 Tsp. Lemon juice
¼ Cup Cheddar cheese, grated, or dry cheese, rehydrated or Parmesan
4 Bread slices or 2 English muffins, split
1 Tb. Onion, minced, rehydrated

Toast bread or English muffins and preheat broiler. Combine tuna, mayonnaise, lemon, onion and cheese. Top bread with tuna mixture and broil until cheese is bubbly.

Tuna Chowder
Serves 4

1 Can Tuna
2 Tbs. Butter
1 Onion, chopped, or ½ Cup dry, rehydrated
1 ½ Cup Potatoes, peeled and diced, either canned or dry and rehydrated
1 Cup Milk, or dry milk, reconstituted
Salt and pepper, to taste

In a saucepan over medium high heat, sauté onion in butter until softened. Add potatoes and milk, heat until boiling and simmer 10 minutes. Stir in tuna and cook until heated through and serve.

Tuna a la King
Serves 2

1 Can Tuna
1 Onion, or ½ Cup dry onion, rehydrated
2 Tbs. Butter
2 Tbs. Flour
1 ½ Cup Milk, or dry milk, reconstituted
1 Cup Peas canned, frozen, or dry rehydrated
2 Tbs. Parmesan cheese, grated, or dry cheese, rehydrated
Salt and pepper, to taste

In a saucepan over medium high heat, sauté onion in butter until softened. Stir in flour, then add milk and stir until thickened. Stir in peas, then tuna and cheese; continue cooking 3 minutes more. Season, then serve over toast, noodles or rice.

Tuna Macaroni
Serves 2

½ lb. Pasta
1 Can Tuna
¼ Cup Olive oil
¼ Tsp. Red pepper flakes
Salt and pepper, to taste

Combine all ingredients and serve.

Tuna Noodle Casserole
Serves 4

2 Cans Tuna
¼ lb. Egg noodles or macaroni
3 Tb. Butter
3 Tb. Flour
2 Cup Milk, or dry milk, reconstituted
3/4 Cup Cheddar cheese, grated, or dry cheese, rehydrated or Parmesan
4 Tb. Olives, black or green, chopped
Salt and pepper, to taste
½ Cup Bread crumbs

Preheat oven to 350. Prepare pasta according to package directions and drain. Meanwhile, in a saucepan over medium high heat sauté butter and flour together. Add Milk, or dry milk, reconstituted, stirring constantly until thickened. Remove from heat and stir in cheese, salt and pepper. Combine noodles, sauce, tuna and olives and pour into a baking dish. Top with crumbs and bake at 350 until bubbly; about 20 minutes.

Tuna and Beans
Serves 4

1 Can Tuna
1 Can Cannellini beans, 15 Oz.
½ Cup Onion, minced or shallots
2/3 Cups Celery, minced
4 Tb. Vinaigrette

Combine all ingredients and serve.

Bulgur and Tuna Salad
Serves 2

2/3 Cups Bulgur
2 Cup Hot water
1 Can Tuna
4 Tb. Vinaigrette
Optional: chopped celery, onion, olives, shallots, etc.

Soak bulgur in water for 40 minutes. Combine with remaining ingredients and serve.

Linguine With Tonnato Sauce
Serves 4

1 lb. thin linguine
1 Can tuna, packed in oil, undrained
½ Cup mayonnaise
¼ Cup olive oil
1 tsp. garlic
¼ Cup drained capers, divided
4 flat anchovy fillets
3 Tbs. lemon juice
2 Tbs. water
1 Cup dry spinach, rehydrated - optional

Boil linguine in salted water according to package directions, about 8 – 10 minutes. Drain, reserving ½ cup of pasta water. Purée tuna with oil from can, mayonnaise, olive oil, 3 tablespoon capers, anchovies, lemon juice, and 2 Tb. water in a blender until smooth. Season with salt and pepper.

Coarsely chop remaining tablespoon capers. Toss hot linguine with sauce, spinach, and remaining tablespoon capers. Thin with some of cooking water, if needed.

Tuna Croquettes

Serves 2

1 Can Tuna, 6 Oz.
⅓ Cup Crackers, crushed
2 Tbs. Onion, minced
1 Egg white or dry egg white, rehydrated
½ Tsp. Dijon mustard
2 Tbs. Olive oil

Preheat a skillet over medium high heat. Meanwhile, mix together all except the olive oil, breaking up the tuna well and form into small patties. Pan fry in olive oil until browned and heated through.

Tip:

Be sure to store plenty of tools to start a fire. Plan on two boxes of matches per month, as well as butane lighters, and flint style fire lighting devices. They are so inexpensive now, but they will be invaluable if you need them.

Seafood, Salmon

Salmon Croquettes
Serves 2

1 Can Salmon, 6 Oz.
⅓ Cup Crackers, crushed
2 Tbs. Onion, minced
1 Egg white, or dry egg equivalent
½ Tsp. Dijon mustard
2 Tbs. Olive oil

Preheat a skillet over medium high heat. Meanwhile, mix together all ingredients except the olive oil, breaking up the salmon well and form into small patties. Pan fry in olive oil until browned and heated through.

Salmon Chowder
Serves 8

1 Can Diced potatoes 15 oz., drained or 2 C dry potatoes, rehydrated
1 Can Diced carrots 15 oz., drained or 2 C dry carrots, rehydrated
1 Can Creamed corn – 15 oz.
2 tsp. dehydrated onion
1 tsp. garlic powder
1 tsp. salt
1 tsp. pepper
1 tsp. dill, dry
2 Cups chicken stock
1 Can evaporated milk, 15 oz. or equivalent dry milk reconstituted with less water
1 cans Salmon 16 oz.
½ lb. dehydrated cheddar cheese

In a large pot, heat stock. Add remaining ingredients except cheese and heat until almost boiling. Turn off heat and stir in cheese. Stir until cheese is incorporated and serve.

Vegetables and Fruit

Broccoli Cheddar Soup
Serves 4

1 ½ Cup Cheddar cheese, grated, rehydrated
1 Can Stock 12.5 Oz., Chicken or beef
2 Tbs. Butter
3 Tb. Flour
⅓ Cup Onion, grated, or dry rehydrated
1 ½ Cups dry broccoli, rehydrated
1 ½ Cup Milk, or dry milk, reconstituted
¼ Tsp. Cayenne pepper, ground

In a saucepan, melt butter and sauté flour 2 minutes. Whisk in onion, stock and cook 2 minutes. Add milk, broccoli and cayenne. Stir until thickened. Stir in cheese until melted and serve.

Potato Leek Soup
Serves 4

1 ¼ Cup Potato flakes
1 Tb. Butter
2 Green onion bunches, chopped or dry onion rehydrated
1 quart Chicken broth, 32 Oz. (4 cups)
1 Cup Milk, or dry milk, reconstituted
¼ Tsp. Pepper

In saucepan, cook onions in butter for 2 minutes. Add broth, Milk, or dry milk, reconstituted and pepper. Stir in potato flakes. Puree and serve.

Cream of Broccoli Soup
Serves 4

4 Cups Chicken Stock or soup base with water
3 Cups Dry Broccoli, steeped in hot water, water reserved
1/3 Cup Dry Diced Onion, rehydrated
2 Tb. Flour
2 Tb. Butter, softened
1 Can Evaporated Milk, 5 oz.
1 ½ Tsp. Lemon Juice

In a large pot, heat chicken stock. Add broccoli and onion. Heat to simmering. Mix together butter and flour and add to the pot. Sir in. Add milk. Simmer until the broccoli is tender, about 20 – 30 minutes. Add the lemon juice. Stir until heated through and serve.

Corn Pancakes
Serves 4

1 Cup Flour
½ Cup Cornmeal
1 heaping TB.. Baking powder
1 TB. Sugar
1 Tsp. Salt
1 Cup Milk, or dry milk, reconstituted
2 Egg, beaten or dry egg equivalent
1 Cup Corn, frozen, canned or dry rehydrated
2 Tbs. Butter or oil

Preheat a greased skillet or griddle over medium high heat. In a bowl, combine dry ingredients. Then add Milk, or dry milk, reconstituted, egg, butter and corn. Pan fry on one side until bubbling, then flip and cook until golden and serve.

Mushroom and Barley Soup
Serves 6

3 Cup Dry Mushrooms
8 Cups Chicken Stock or Soup Base with water
¼ Cup Oil
1 Cup dry diced Onion, rehydrated
1 Cup dry Carrots, rehydrated
3 Tsp. Garlic
½ Cup Pearl Barley
1 ¼ tsp. Salt
¼ Tsp. dry Thyme

In a large pot, add mushrooms, and stock and heat to a simmer. In a skillet, heat oil and add rehydrated onion and carrots and cook over medium heat, stirring, about 5 minutes. Add garlic and cook 3 minute more. Add the onion mixture, barley, salt and thyme to the soup pot and simmer until the barley is tender, about 50 minutes.

Blender Salsa

1- 14 oz. can diced tomatoes
1- 10 oz. can rotel tomatoes
¼ Cup dry onion, rehydrated
1 tsp. garlic
½ tsp. red pepper flakes or 1 jalapeno, diced
1 tsp. honey
1/2 tsp. salt
1/4 tsp. ground cumin
2 TB dry cilantro
2 Tb. Lemon juice

Whirls all ingredients in a blender.

Tuscan Tomato and Bread Soup

Serves 6

¼ Cup Olive oil
1 Cup dry Onion
3 Tsp. garlic
6 Cups Chicken Stock or soup base and water
2 cans, tomatoes, 28 oz. each, crushed by hand
1 loaf stale bread, cubed
2 tsp. dry basil
Salt and pepper

In a large pot, sauté onion in oil until soft. Add garlic and cook 3 minutes. A stock and tomatoes. Simmer 20 minutes. Add bread, basil, salt and pepper. Simmer 15 minutes. Using a whisk, stir to break up bread. Serve.

Potato Pancakes

Serves 4

6 Potatoes, medium, grated, or dry hash browns, rehydrated
4 Egg whites, beaten stiff, or equivalent dry egg product
4 Egg yolks or equivalent dry egg product
4 Tb. Flour
4 Tb. Evaporated Milk, or dry milk, reconstituted
1 ½ Tsp. Salt
Butter for griddle
Salt and pepper, to taste

Combine egg yolks, flour, evaporated Milk, or dry milk, reconstituted, and salt in mixing bowl. Fold in cheese, and potatoes then fold in beaten egg whites. Grease hot griddle with butter. Place batter on griddle with slotted spoon. Cook both sides until golden brown. Serve with salt and pepper.

Ambrosia Salad
Serves 6

1 Cup Coconut, sweetened flaked
1 Can Mandarin oranges, 11 Oz.
1 Can Pineapple crushed
1 Cup Sour cream, sour cream powder, reconstituted
1 Cup Mini marshmallows
½ Cup Pecans, toasted and chopped

Combine in medium bowl and serve.

Russian Potato Salad
Serves 4

4 Cups dry potato cubes, rehydrated
2 Eggs, or dry egg equivalent, reconstituted, hard cooked and diced
¼ Cup Pickles, diced
1 Cup Peas, canned or dry, rehydrated
1 ½ Cup Mayonnaise
1 Tsp. Dill, dried
1 ½ Cup Mayonnaise
Optional: Diced ham, cooked chicken or shrimp, diced

Combine all ingredients and serve.

Groundnut (Peanut) Soup

Serves 6

1 Tb. vegetable oil
1 ½ Cups rehydrated dry diced onion
½ Cup rehydrated, chopped carrots, minced
3 Cups rehydrated sweet potato
3 Cups water
1 Can condensed tomato soup, 10.75-ounce
1/2 Cup creamy peanut butter
1 teaspoon curry powder
1/8 to 1/4 teaspoon cayenne pepper
1/2 cup reconstituted sour cream (optional)
2 tablespoons chopped peanuts, for garnish (optional)

Heat the oil in a large saucepan over medium heat. Add the onion and the carrot and sauté until tender, about 3 to 5 minutes.

Add the sweet potato and the water, then cover and simmer for 10 minutes or until the sweet potato is soft. Stir in the condensed soup, peanut butter, curry, and cayenne pepper, then bring the mixture to a boil. Remove the pan from the heat and let cool for 10 minutes.

Puree the soup in a blender in 2 batches (optional), then return it to the pan and reheat it. Ladle the soup into bowls and, if you like, top it with a drizzle of sour cream and a few chopped peanuts.

Corn and Potato Chowder

Serves 6

2 tablespoons butter, margarine or shortening
1 Cup rehydrated dry diced onion
½ Cup rehydrated dry celery
5 ½ Cups chicken stock or chicken bouillon
1 ½ cups rehydrated dry corn kernels
1 ½ Cup rehydrated dry potato, diced
½ teaspoon salt, to taste
1 Can evaporated milk, 5 oz.
3 tablespoons all-purpose flour
Black pepper, to taste
Fresh dill or parsley for garnish, chopped

Melt the butter in a large saucepan or medium soup pot. Stir in the onion and celery.

Partially cover the pan and cook the vegetables over moderate heat for 9 to 10 minutes, stirring occasionally. Add the chicken stock, corn, potato, and salt and bring the mixture to a low boil. Lower the heat, cover the pot, and simmer for about 7 minutes, until the potatoes are just tender.

In a small bowl, whisk together the cream and flour. Stir the mixture into the soup with the pepper. Bring the soup back to a low boil, then reduce the heat and simmer for about 8 minutes. Serve hot, sprinkled with herbs.

Tip:

Remember to store extras of all your sundries. Remember the saying, one is none, two is one. If stores are closed, you need to be your own store.

Pasta

Penne all'amatriciana
Serves 4

8 Oz. Penne pasta
4 Oz. Pancetta or bacon, cubed
1 Cup Onion, chopped or ¼ C dried onion, rehydrated or dehydrated onion, reconstituted
1 Tb. Garlic, minced or dry garlic, rehydrated
1 Cup Diced tomatoes, 28 Oz.
Salt and pepper, to taste
1 Tsp. Red chili flakes
¼ Cup Parmesan cheese

Boil pasta in salted water until al dente; drain. Fry meat over med high heat until half cooked. Drain pan. Add onion and garlic cooking 5 minutes. Add tomatoes, salt and pepper and red chili flakes. Cook 10 minutes to reduce juices. Add pasta. Spoon onto serving plates and garnish with Parmesan.

Tortellini and Black Bean Soup
Serves 8

3 tablespoons olive oil
1 medium onion, chopped
1 garlic clove, crushed
1 cup canned chopped tomatoes, drained
8 cups canned low-salt chicken broth
1 teaspoon each dried oregano and basil
3 15-ounce cans black beans, rinsed and drained
2 tablespoons rice vinegar
Black pepper, to taste
12 ounces dried cheese tortellini

In a large soup pot, heat the olive oil over medium heat. Add the onion and sauté for 3 minutes. Add the garlic and drained tomatoes and cook for 3 minutes. Add the chicken broth, oregano, basil, drained black beans, vinegar, and black pepper to taste.

Reduce the heat to low and simmer for 5 minutes. Add the tortellini to the soup and cook for 8 minutes or until tender.

Tortellini with Mushroom Sauce

1 ounce dried mushrooms
2 8-ounce packages dried three-cheese tortellini
2 tablespoons butter
½ Cup dry diced onion, rehydrated
1 tsp. thyme, divided
1 small can evaporated milk
3/4 cup grated Parmesan cheese, divided

Place mushrooms in 2-cup measuring cup; add enough hot water to measure 2 cups. Let stand until mushrooms are soft, about 20 minutes. Drain mushrooms, reserving soaking liquid. Coarsely chop mushrooms.

Cook tortellini in large pot of boiling salted water until just tender, stirring occasionally. Meanwhile, melt butter in large skillet over medium-high heat. Add onion; sauté until golden and tender, about 4 minutes. Add mushrooms and thyme; sauté 2 minutes.

Stir in 1 cup mushroom soaking liquid and evaporation milk. Boil until thickened to light sauce consistency, about 3 minutes. Season to taste with salt and pepper. Drain tortellini; return to same pot. Add mushroom mixture and toss to coat. Stir in 1/2 cup cheese. Season with salt and pepper. Transfer tortellini to bowl; sprinkle with 1/4 cup cheese.

Tortellini Vegetable Soup
Serves 4

2 tablespoons olive oil
1 Cup dried diced onion, rehydrated
1 Cup dehydrated corn kernels, rehydrated
1 Cup dry carrots, rehydrated
1 quart Chicken stock
1 ½ Cups water
1 teaspoon dried basil
1 bay leaf
1 Can canned crushed tomatoes – 14.5 oz.
1/2 teaspoon salt
8 to 9 ounces dried tortellini
1 Tb. dried parsley
Black pepper, to taste

Heat the olive oil in a medium soup pot or large saucepan. Add the onion, corn, and carrot. Sauté over medium heat for 8 to 10 minutes. Add the remaining ingredients and simmer until tortellini are tender.

Stovetop Mac and Cheese
Serves 6

1½ lb. Elbow macaroni
6 Cup Extra sharp cheddar, grated, or dry cheese, rehydrated or Parmesan
2 Cup Half and half (or Milk, or dry milk, reconstituted)
4 Tb. Butter
1 Tb. Dijon mustard
1 ½ Tsp. Salt
1 Tsp. Pepper, fresh ground
3/4 Tsp. Hot sauce, optional

Boil pasta in salted water until al dente; drain. Return pasta to pot over low heat; add remaining . Cook and stir until cheese is melted and sauce thickens.

Spaghetti Pie
Serves 4

6 Oz. Spaghetti, cooked and still warm
2 Tbs. Butter
1 Egg, beaten or equivalent dry egg, rehydrated
⅓ Cup Parmesan cheese
1 Cup Cottage cheese or ricotta or jarred alfredo sauce
1 Cup Mozzarella cheese, grated, or dry cheese, rehydrated
1 Can Spaghetti sauce, 28 Oz.

Combine hot cooked spaghetti with butter until butter is melted. Add egg and Parmesan cheese. Place in pie dish, and form a "crust" with a well in the center. Spread cottage cheese over spaghetti in pie dish. Cover with spaghetti sauce, and sprinkle with mozzarella cheese. Bake 30 minutes at 350°F or until bubbly. Cut into slices and serve.

Spaghetti with Clams
Serves 2

1 Can Clams, 6.5 Oz.
½ lb. Spaghetti noodles
¼ Cup Olive oil
2 Tsp. Garlic, minced
Red pepper flakes, to taste

Prepare spaghetti according to package directions and drain. Meanwhile, in skillet over medium heat, sauté garlic in oil until golden. Drain clam juices into skillet, increase heat and simmer. Add clams when spaghetti is ready and heat through. Season and serve pasta topped with sauce.

Sesame Noodles and Peas
Serves 8

1 lb. Linguine
2 Tbs. Chili sesame oil
⅓ Cup Soy sauce
2 Tbs. Brown sugar
2 Tbs. Balsamic vinegar
1 Tb. Ginger, fresh, grated, or 1 tsp. dried ginger
½ Cup Sesame seeds, toasted
2 Cup Peas, frozen

Start a pot of water boiling and cook the linguine according to package directions, adding the peas for the final minute of cooking time. Meanwhile whisk together the remaining . When the linguine and peas are done, drain them well, toss with the sauce, and serve.

Linguine with Anchovy and Tomato Sauce
Serves 6

1 lb. Linguine
1 Can Tomatoes, 28 Oz., chopped and drained
2 Tbs. Olive oil
1 Tsp. Garlic, minced
6 Anchovy fillets, with some of their oil
Salt and pepper, to taste

Bring a pot of salted water to a boil. Place the oil in a deep skillet over medium heat. Add garlic and anchovies after one minute. When garlic sizzles and anchovies break apart, add tomatoes. Turn heat to medium high, bringing to a boil. Cook until mixture becomes saucy, about 15 minutes, stirring occasionally. Cook pasta. Season sauce to taste, and serve over the linguine.

Gnocchi with Sundried Tomatoes and Artichokes
Serves 6

1 package Tricolor or white gnocchi, 16 Oz.
¼ Cup Olive oil
¼ Tsp. Red pepper flakes, to taste
1 Tsp. Garlic, minced
½ Cup Marinated sun-dried tomatoes, drained and cut into pieces
1 Can Artichoke hearts, 14 Oz., drained and quartered
2 tsp. dried basil
½ Cup Gouda cheese, grated, or dry cheese, rehydrated or Parmesan or diced

Prepare gnocchi according to the package. In a skillet, heat oil. Add the red pepper and garlic, cooking for 1 minute. Add the tomatoes and artichokes; sauté them over medium low heat for 7 to 10 minutes. Drain the gnocchi, and add it to the skillet along with the basil. Stir to combine, and heat through. Transfer to a serving plate, and top with cheese. Stir together, and serve.

Pasta with Cannellini Beans
Serves 8

2 Tbs. Olive oil
2 Tsp. Garlic, minced
1 Can Diced tomatoes, 28 Oz.
2 Cans Cannellini beans, 15 Oz.
1 package Farfalle or other short pasta, 16 Oz.
1 tsp. dried basil
Salt and pepper, to taste
Parmesan cheese, grated

Heat the oil and garlic, in a large skillet over medium heat. When garlic begins to sizzle add the tomatoes and beans and all their liquid. Bring to a low boil and simmer for about 20 minutes, or until the pasta is ready. Prepare the pasta according to package instructions. Add the basil to the tomato sauce about a minute or two before you drain the pasta. Season with salt and pepper. Drain the pasta and add to the sauce, stir to mix well. Serve the pasta topped with lots of Parmesan cheese.

Asian Sesame Noodles with Peanut Sauce
Serves 4

1 lb. Spaghetti
2 Tsp. garlic, minced
1 jalapeno, seeded and minced or 2 tsp. red pepper flakes
½ Cup peanut butter
¼ Cup rice vinegar
¼ C soy sauce
1 Tb. Sesame oil
1/3 Cup hot water

Cook the spaghetti according to package directions, then drain and return to the pot. While the spaghetti is cooking, blend the remaining ingredients in a blender or whisk together in a bowl. Add sauce to warm noodles and stir to combine.

Spaghetti with Olive Oil and Garlic
Serves 2

½ lb. Spaghetti noodles
¼ Cup Olive oil
1 Tb. Garlic, minced
Red pepper flakes

Boil spaghetti until al dente; about 10 minutes and drain. Meanwhile, in a small skillet, sauté garlic in olive oil. Toss pasta with oil and garlic, and season to taste with pepper flakes.

Pasta Marinara
Serves 2

½ lb. Pasta, whole wheat
½ Tb. Olive oil
2 Tsp. Garlic, minced
1 Can Diced tomatoes 14 Oz.
½ Tsp. Thyme, dried
Salt and pepper, to taste
1 Tb. Parmesan cheese, grated

Cook the pasta in boiling water until al dente and drain. Meanwhile heat the oil in a skillet over medium high heat. Add garlic and sauté briefly. Add remaining and simmer 10 minutes. Serve sauce over pasta.

Cheesy Meximac
Serves 4

8 Oz. Rotini pasta
1 Green onion, or 2 Tbs. minced onion, rehydrated
½ Tb. Butter
½ Tb. Flour
3/4 Cup Milk, or dry milk, reconstituted
Salt and pepper, to taste
8 Oz. Pepper jack cheese, grated, or dry cheese, rehydrated or Parmesan
1 Can Mexican flavored corn, 10 Oz.
Dash Chili powder

Preheat oven to 350°. Boil pasta in salted water until al dente, adding scallions the last two minutes of cooking drain; set aside. Melt butter, whisk in flour, add Milk, or dry milk, reconstituted, chili powder, salt and pepper stirring until smooth. Simmer 4 minutes. Remove from heat and add half of the cheese. Add corn then combine with pasta. Pour half of mixture into 9 x 9 inch pan coated nonstick spray. Add remaining pasta then remaining cheese. Bake 25 minutes. Allow to stand 5 minutes before serving.

Linguine with Shrimp and Feta
Serves 8

1 lb. Linguine
1 lb. Shrimp, medium, peeled and deveined or 1 pint canned shrimp
1 Tsp. Olive oil
½ Tsp. Oregano, dried
½ Tsp. Salt
¼ Tsp. Red pepper flakes, to taste
2 Tsp. Garlic, minced
½ Cup Dry white wine, chicken stock or water
1 Can Tomatoes, chopped, 14 Oz.
3/4 Cup Feta cheese, dried and reconstituted or Parmesan

Preheat the oven to 350. Start a pot of water and boil the linguine according to package and drain. Spray a baking dish with cooking spray. While the pasta is cooking, in a large skillet over medium high heat cook shrimp in oil with the oregano, garlic, salt and red pepper for about 3 minutes. Pour into the prepared baking dish. Add the wine or stock or water to the empty skillet and cook until reduced by half, about 3 minutes. Add tomatoes and pour over shrimp. Sprinkle the dish with feta and bake 10 minutes. Serve shrimp over linguine.

Spicy Shrimp Pasta with Olives
Serves 4

1 lb. Shrimp, medium, peeled and deveined or 1 pint canned shrimp
1 lb. Fettuccine
1 ½ Cup Olives, pitted
4 Tsp. Garlic, minced
3 Tb. Olive oil
2 Tbs. Parsley, dried
¼ Tsp. Red pepper flakes
¼ Cup Parmesan cheese, grated

Bring a large pot of salted water to boil covered and cook pasta according to package. Add shrimp for the last 5 minutes. Chop olives. In a skillet, heat olive oil. Add garlic, olives, parsley and red pepper flakes. Add cooked shrimp and pasta, toss to combine. Sprinkle with cheese and serve.

Ultra Creamy Macaroni and Cheese
Serves 8

1 lb. Macaroni
1 Tsp. Salt
6 Tb. Butter
1 Tsp. Mustard, powdered
1 Tsp. Garlic, minced
¼ Tsp. Cayenne pepper, ground
6 Tb. Flour
1 Can Chicken stock,   14.5 Oz.
3 ½ Cup Milk, or dry milk, reconstituted
1 lb. Colby cheese, grated, or dry Colby cheese, rehydrated
½ lb. Extra sharp cheddar, grated, or dry cheddar cheese, rehydrated or equivalent processed cheese food - velveeta
Black pepper, to taste
4 Bread slices, torn
2 Tbs. Butter, melted

Start a large pot of water to boil, and add the teaspoon of salt to the water. Preheat the oven to 400, and position a rack in the center of the oven. Spray a 9 X 13 pan with cooking spray.
When the water boils, add the macaroni and boil until just al dente, about 5 minutes. Drain well. Wipe out the pot and reduce the heat to medium. Add the butter, spices, and garlic. Stir in the flour, whisking out any lumps. Cook 2 minutes, then slowly stir in the chicken stock and Milk, or dry milk, reconstituted. Stir until thickened, about 6 to 9 minutes. Remove from the heat; whisk in the grated, or dry cheese, rehydrated or Parmesan cheese, stirring until melted. Season with salt and pepper, then stir in macaroni. To make crumb topping: in a food processor, chop the bread into fine crumbs, then stir in melted butter. Pour the macaroni and cheese into the baking dish, top with bread crumb mixture, cover with foil, and bake 25, 30 minutes. Remove the foil, and bake until golden, 20, 25 minutes more.

Potato Gnocchi
Serves 8

2 Cup dry potato flakes
2 cup boiling water
2 Egg, beaten or equivalent powder, reconstituted
2 tsp. salt
¼ tsp. ground black pepper
1 ½ Cups flour
2 Tb. Butter
2 Cups Spaghetti sauce, warmed
¼ Cup Parmesan cheese

Place potato flakes in a medium-size bowl. Pour in boiling water; stir until blended. Let cool.

Stir in egg, salt, and pepper. Blend in enough flour to make a fairly stiff dough. Turn dough out on a well-floured board. Knead lightly.

Divide dough in quarters. Shape each half into a long roll, about 5/8 " wide. Cut into bite-size pieces. Gently roll each gnocchi over the tines of a fork leaving the imprint of the ridges and a dimple from you fingertip.

Bring a pot of salted water to a boil and cook the gnocchi several at a time in gently simmering water.

As gnocchi rise to the top of the pot, remove them with a slotted spoon to a dish. Repeat until all are cooked. Add the butter to the gnocchi and mix gently. Meanwhile, warm the spaghetti sauce. Add the spaghetti sauce to the gnocchi, and serve sprinkled with Parmesan cheese.

Tip:

Another great way to sauce gnocchi is to brown some butter and toss to coat.

Beef

Beef Noodle Soup
Serves 8

2 Quarts Beef Stock (8 Cups) or soup base and water
½ Cup Dry Onion
½ Cup Dry Carrots
½ Cup Dry Celery
½ Tsp. Dry Thyme
1 Cup Canned Diced Tomato
2 Cups Egg Noodles or other pasta
2 Pints Canned Beef Chunks, shredded
2 Tb. Dry Parsley
Salt and Pepper to taste

In a soup pot, bring the beef stock to a simmer and add onion, carrots, celery, thyme, and tomatoes. Cook until vegetables are tender, about 20 minutes. Add pasta, and cook until tender, about 8 minutes. Add beef, parsley, salt and pepper, and simmer until heated through, about 5 minutes. Serve.

Beef Barley Soup with Mushrooms
Serves 8

2 Quarts Beef Stock (8 Cups) or soup base and water
½ Cup Dry Onion
½ Cup Dry Carrots
½ Cup Dry Celery
1 Cup Dry Mushrooms
½ Tsp. Dry Thyme
1 Cup Canned Diced Tomato
1 Cup Barley
2 Pints Canned Beef Chunks, shredded
2 Tb. Dry Parsley
Salt and Pepper to taste

In a soup pot, bring the beef stock to a simmer and add onion, carrots, celery, thyme, tomatoes and barley. Cook until barley are tender, about 45 minutes. Add beef, parsley, salt and pepper, and simmer until heated through, about 5 minutes. Serve.

BBQ Shepherd's Pie
Serves 4

1 ¼ Cup Ground beef or 1 pint canned ground beef
1 Onion, medium, chopped, or ½ Cup dried onion, rehydrated
1 Chili beans, 15 Oz.
3/4 Cup Barbecue sauce
Potato flakes, prepared according to package for 4 servings.

Preheat broiler. Heat an oven proof skillet to med high. Cook ground beef and onion for 8 minutes until beef is heated through and no longer pink; drain. Add drained beans and bbq sauce. Simmer 8 minutes. Prepare potatoes; spread on top of meat mix. Broil for 6 minutes until potatoes are golden.

Swedish Meatballs
Serves 6

2 pints canned meatballs
2 Tb. Butter or shortening
2 Tb. Flour
1 Cup chicken or beef stock or bouillon, prepared.
1/3 Cup Jelly, for serving

In a skillet warm meatballs in melted butter. Sprinkle in flour and stir to distribute. Add stock and cook until heated through and sauce is thickened. Serve with jelly.

Meatball Alphabet Soup
Serves 6

1 Pint canned meatballs
2 tablespoons olive oil
½ Cup dried diced onion, rehydrated
½ Cup dried celery, rehydrated
1 tsp. garlic
1 quart chicken stock
1 cup crushed canned tomatoes in puree, 28 oz.
Heat the oil in a large saucepan. Add the onion, celery, and garlic. Partially cover the pan and cook the vegetables over medium heat for 10 minutes, stirring occasionally. Add the chicken stock, crushed tomatoes, and spices. Bring the soup to a simmer over medium-low heat, then add the pasta.

Simmer the soup until the pasta is almost cooked, then add the meatballs to the pot and simmer gently for 3 minutes more to heat through.

Nanny's Meatballs
Serves 4

1 pint canned meatballs
2 Tbs. Cup Oil
3 Cups Spaghetti sauce
½ lb. Rigatoni, cooked

Heat oil over medium heat. Brown Meatballs until heated through - 5 minutes. Drain off any excess fat. Add spaghetti sauce and simmer for about 20 minutes. Meanwhile, cook pasta in boiling water until done. Serve sauce over pasta with additional cheese as garnish.

Saucy Asian Meatballs
Serves 6

2 pints canned meatballs
3 Tb. Soy sauce, divided
¼ Cup Rice wine vinegar or apple cider
¼ Cup Tomato paste or 4 Tb tomato powder mixed with water
2 Tbs. Molasses
1 Tsp. Hot sauce

Combine in saucepan: vinegar, tomato paste, molasses, hot sauce and remaining soy sauce. Cook 4 minutes. Add meatballs. Heat to serving temperature then serve with steamed rice.

Mom's Lasagna
Serves 6

2 lb. Ground beef or 2 pints canned ground beef
1 Can Tomato sauce
6 Lasagna noodles
2 Cup Cottage cheese, ricotta or 1 Cup Alfredo sauce
2 Eggs, or dry egg equivalent, reconstituted
Parmesan cheese
3 Cups Mozzarella cheese, grated
½ Tb. Garlic salt
½ Tb. Oregano

For raw beef, cook and drain. Cook lasagna noodles in boiling water. Preheat oven to 350°. In a large bowl mix ground beef, oregano, garlic salt, and tomato sauce. In another bowl mix together cottage cheese, ricotta or alfredo sauce and eggs. Layer meat parmesan cheese, cottage cheese mix, mozzarella cheese, noodles in pan. Top layer should be mozzarella cheese. Bake until bubbly, about 30 minutes.

Tamale Pie
Serves 8

Filling:
2 Tb. Butter, margarine or shortening
2 Pints canned beef (ground or chunks or combination of both)
¼ Cup Chili powder
1 tsp. Cumin
1 Cup dry chopped onion, rehydrated
½ C dry green bell pepper, rehydrated
½ C dry Celery, rehydrated
2 tsp. garlic
Salt and pepper
1 can crushed tomatoes, 28 oz.
1 ½ Cup dehydrated corn kernels, rehydrated or 1 can of corn
1 Can black olives, chopped
3 jalapeno chilies, minced or 2 Tb. red pepper flakes

Cornmeal mixture:
1 Cup cornmeal
1 Cup water
3 ½ Cups chicken broth (or water)
2 tps. Salt
4 Tb. Butter, margarine or lard
1 ½ C grated cheddar, dry, rehydrated – optional

In a large skillet, heat butter and add beef, breaking up any clumps. Add remaining ingredients. Simmer 20 minutes. Add cornmeal, water, broth, and salt and stir over low heat for about 40 minutes stirring frequently. Add butter. Meanwhile, preheat the oven to 350. In a large baking dish, add half the cornmeal mixture and smooth to spread out. Add the meat mixture, and then the remaining cornmeal. Top with cheese, if using. bake 30 minutes.

Mexican Casserole
Serves 8

¼ C shortening, oil or lard
8 Flour Tortillas
2 pints canned ground beef
3 Cups Salsa
1 Can black beans, 14.5 oz., drained
1 Cup cheese, dry reconstituted or ½ C Parmesan - optional
1 Cup dry sour cream, reconstituted

Preheat oven to 350°. In a skillet, heat 2 Tb. Shortening and toast the tortillas until crisp, one at a time, or coat them in oil, and toast them in the oven until crisp adding more oil shortening as needed. Tear toasted tortillas into 2" pieces and layer in a baking dish. To the skillet, add the ground beef, and reheat, breaking up any chunks. Layer over tortillas in the baking dish. Add more shortening to the pan, add the salsa and beans and cook, stirring, 10 minutes. Spoon the salsa over the beef and tortillas, drizzle with reconstituted sour cream and top with cheese, if using. Heat the dish in the oven until heated through and bubbly.

Meat and Potatoes Hot Dish
Serves 8

4 Tb. Butter or oil, divided
2 tsp. Garlic
1 Cup Onion, diced, dry and reconstituted
2 Pints canned beef, chunks or ground
2 ½ Cups Alfredo sauce
2 C Potatoes, sliced, dry and rehydrated
1 C Peas, dry and rehydrated
½ C Parmesan cheese
2 Cups Bread crumbs

Preheat oven to 350°. In 2 Tb. butter or oil, cook rehydrated onion and garlic until fragrant. Add beef and stir to warm and chop up. Layer beef mixture in the bottom of a baking dish. Top with half the alfredo sauce, then layer on potatoes and peas. Top with remaining alfredo sauce. Toast bread crumbs in the remaining 2 Tb. butter. Sprinkle on top of the casserole. Sprinkle on the Parmesan. Bake until bubbly, about 30 minutes.

Cheeseburger and Fries Casserole
Serves 8

1 lb. Ground Beef or 1 pint canned ground beef
3 Cups Frozen or dried rehydrated potato nuggets, tator-tots or dried, shredded potatoes, rehydrated
1 Can Tomato sauce, 16 Oz.
1 Cup Onion, chopped or ¼ C dried onion, rehydrated or ¼ Cup dried, rehydrated onion
2 Tsp. Italian seasoning
1 Tsp. salt
½ Tsp. Pepper
2 Cups Cheddar cheese, grated, or dry cheese, rehydrated or Parmesan

Preheat Oven to 350. Coat a 9x13 pan with cooking spray. For raw beef, in a large Skillet cook ground beef until brown; drain off fat. Place Potato Nuggets in the bottom of the prepped baking dish; top with cooked or canned ground beef. Stir together tomato sauce, onion, Italian herbs, salt and pepper; pour over ground beef. Sprinkle with cheese. Bake uncovered about 40 minutes or until hot and bubbly

Cheesy Beefaroni
Serves 8

1 Tsp. Vegetable oil
1 Cup Onion, chopped or ¼ C dried onion, rehydrated or ¼ dehydrated onion, reconstituted
2 Tsp. Garlic, minced
3/4 lb. Ground beef, lean
1 3/4 Cup Spaghetti sauce
2 Cup Chicken or beef stock, divided
¼ Cup Flour
2 Cup Milk, or dry milk, reconstituted
1 Cup Cheddar cheese, grated, or dry cheese, rehydrated
½ Cup Mozzarella cheese, grated, or dry cheese, rehydrated
2 Tbs. Parmesan cheese, grated,
1 lb. Macaroni

Preheat the oven to 450. Spray a 9 X 13 baking dish with cooking spray. Start a large pot of salted water to boil for the pasta. When boiling, add pasta cooking until al dente; drain, and reserve. Meanwhile, in a skillet over medium high heat, cook onions and garlic in oil until softened, 4 minutes. Add beef, and cook until no longer pink, breaking up clumps. Add spaghetti sauce and ½ Cup stock. Cover, and simmer 10 minutes. Meanwhile, in a large saucepan, whisk together Milk, or dry milk, reconstituted, flour, and remaining stock. Bring to a boil over medium heat, stirring periodically until thickened. Remove from heat, and stir in cheese. Stir together pasta, meat mixture, and cheese mixture until well combined. Pour into the baking dish, sprinkle with mozzarella and Parmesan, and bake until bubbly, about 10 minutes.

Light TexMex Beef and Bean Soup
Serves 6

2 Tsp. Vegetable oil
1 Cup Onion, chopped or ¼ C dried onion, rehydrated
2 Tsp. Garlic, minced
½ lb. Ground beef, lean
1 Can Tomatoes, diced, 15 Oz.
1 Can Kidney beans, 15 Oz., drained
1 Can Chicken or beef stock, 14.5 Oz.
1 Can Tomato sauce, 8 Oz.
1 Tsp. Basil, dried
1 Tsp. Chili powder
2 Tsp. Seasoned salt
½ Tsp. Oregano, dried

In a large saucepan over medium high heat, cook onions and garlic in oil until softened, about 5 minutes. Add beef, and cook, breaking up the beef, until no longer pink. Add stock, tomatoes, beans, tomato sauce, and spices. Bring to a boil; then, reduce heat, and simmer about 15 minutes.

Easy Cheeseburger Pie
Serves 4

1 lb. Ground beef, or turkey, or chicken, browned or 1 pint canned ground beef
1 Onion, chopped, or 1 Cup dry, rehydrated
1 Can Green chilies, diced (optional)
½ Tsp. Salt
1 Cup Cheddar cheese, grated, or dry cheese, rehydrated or Parmesan
½ Cup Biscuit mix
1 Cup Milk, or dry milk, reconstituted
2 Eggs, or dry egg equivalent, reconstituted

Preheat oven to 400°F. Brown raw meat or warm canned ground meat and onions, then drain any excess fat. Grease 9 inch pie plate. Spread meat mixture in pie plate; sprinkle with salt, chilies, and cheese. Stir in remaining ingredients until blended. Bake about 25 minutes or until bubbly.

Chili and Frybread
Serves 4

3 Cups Flour
1 tsp. Salt
3 Tb. Shortening
1 Tb. Baking powder
1 ½ Cups Water
2 Cans Chili, 15 oz.
1 pint canned ground beef

Mix the flour, salt, 1 Tb. shortening, baking powder and most of the water and knead. Add more water if needed to make a soft dough. Let rest 10 minutes. Melt the remaining shortening in a skillet. Flatten chunks of dough into small tortillas size pieces. Fry in hot shortening until all fry breads are done. Set aside and keep warm. In the skillet add the beef and break up and chunks. Add the chili and cook until heated through. Serve chili with frybread.

Southwest Beef Stew
Serves 8

1 pint canned ground beef or beef chunks, chopped
1 can corn, 14.5 oz. or 2 Cups dry corn
2 Cups diced potatoes, dry and rehydrated or canned
1 Can black beans, drained
1 Cup Salsa
¾ Cup Water
1 tsp. Cumin
1 tsp. Garlic salt
1 Tb. Chili powder
2 Cups Tomato juice or 1 can tomatoes, 14.5 oz.

Combine all ingredients and simmer 20 minutes.

Slow Cooked Taco Chili
Serves 4

1 lb. Ground beef, or turkey, or chicken or 1 pint canned ground meat
1 package Taco seasoning, 1.25 Oz.
2 Cans Chunky Mexican style tomatoes, 15 Oz. each
1 Can Kidney beans, 15 Oz.
1 Can Corn, whole kernel

Brown or heat ground meat in a large skillet. Drain excess fat. Combine browned meat, taco seasoning, undrained tomatoes, undrained beans, and undrained corn. Cover, and cook in a slow cooker or wonder oven on low for 5 hours.

Beef and Broccoli
Serves 2

½ Cup Flour
1 Can Beef stock, 14 Oz.
2 Tbs. Sugar
2 Tbs. Soy sauce
1 lb. Round steak, cut into 1 inch pieces or 1 pint canned beef chunks
¼ Tsp. Ginger, minced or dry ginger
1 Garlic cloves
4 Cups Broccoli, chopped, fresh, frozen or dried, reconstituted

In a small bowl, combine flour, broth, sugar, and soy sauce. Stir until sugar and flour are dissolved.

In a large skillet or wok over high heat, heat beef, stirring 2 to 4 minutes, or until browned.

Stir in broth mixture, ginger, garlic, and broccoli. Bring to a boil, then reduce heat. Simmer 5 to 10 minutes, or until sauce thickens. This is wonderful served over white rice.

Cuban Beef Picadillo
Serves 4

1 Tb. Olive oil
1 Onions, yellow or ¼ Cup dry onion, rehydrated
1 ½ lb. Ground beef or 1 pint canned ground beef
2 Tsp. Garlic, minced
2 Tbs. Chili powder
3/4 Tsp. Cinnamon
½ Tsp. Allspice, ground
1 Can Diced tomatoes, 28 Oz., undrained
1 3/4 Cup Beef broth
2/3 Cups Raisins or currants
2 Tbs. Tomato paste
¼ Cup Red wine vinegar
Salt and pepper, to taste
Steamed rice for serving

In a large skillet, heat oil over medium high heat; add onion. Sauté until soft and tender, about 4 minutes. Add the beef, and cook until the meat is hot and cooked through. Use a wooden spoon to break up any clumps of meat. Discard any excess fat. Stir in the garlic, chili powder, cinnamon, and allspice. Cook while stirring frequently for 1 minute. Add tomatoes, broth, raisins, paste, and vinegar. Bring to a simmer, and reduce heat to medium. Cook, uncovered, for about 12 to 15 minutes or until slightly thickened, like a stew. Season with salt and pepper. Serve over steamed rice.

Crock Pot Beef and Barley Soup
Serves 6

1 ½ lb. Beef stew meat, cut into 1 inch cubes or 1 pint canned beef chunks
1 Tb. Vegetable oil
1 Cup Carrots, thinly sliced or dry carrots, rehydrated
1 Cup Celery, sliced or dry celery, rehydrated
1 Onion, medium, thinly sliced or dry onion, rehydrated
½ Cup Bell pepper, green, chopped or dry, rehydrated
4 Cup Beef broth
1 Can Tomatoes 14.5 Oz., cut up
1 Cup Spaghetti sauce
1 Cup Pearl barley
1 ½ Tsp. Basil, dried,
½ Tsp. Salt
¼ Tsp. Black pepper
¼ Cup Parsley, fresh, chopped, or 1 Tb. dry optional

For raw beef, in a large skillet, brown meat cubes in oil, half at a time if necessary. Drain oil. Add beef to a crock pot the carrots, celery, onion, green pepper, broth, undrained tomatoes, spaghetti sauce, barley, basil, salt, and pepper. Stir to combine well. Cover, and cook on low in a crock pot, or in a wonder oven for 9 to 10 hours (or 4.5 to 5 hours on crock pot high). Before serving, skim off any fat from the top, and stir in parsley.

Slow Cooked Beef and Vegetable Soup
Serves 4

1 lb. Ground beef, or turkey, or chicken or 1 pint canned beef or chicken
1 Can Beef or chicken broth, 14 Oz.
1 ¼ Cup Water
1 package Mixed vegetables, frozen, 10 Oz. or dry, rehydrated
1 Can Tomatoes, 14.5 Oz., cut up
1 Can Condensed tomato soup, 10.75 Oz.
1 Tb. Dried minced onion
1 Tsp. Italian seasoning,
¼ Tsp. Garlic powder

In a large skillet, brown (or reheat) ground beef. Drain fat away from meat. Put meat and the rest of the ingredients into the crock pot. Cover, and cook on low setting for 7 hours or on high for 3.5 to 4 hours. Alternately bring the ingredients to a boil in a pot with the lid on, then transfer to a wonder oven to slow cook for 5 - 7 hours.

Beef Enchiladas
Serves 4

1 lb. Ground beef or 1 pint beef canned
1 Onion, chopped, or 1 Cup dry, rehydrated
1 Can Enchilada sauce
4 Flour tortillas
2 Cup Cheddar cheese, grated, or dry cheese, rehydrated or Parmesan

In skillet, brown or reheat hamburger and chopped onion. Drain. Pour ¼ c. sauce into the bottom of a baking pan. On each tortilla, place ground beef and sprinkle with cheese. Roll, placing seam side down in baking dish. Pour remaining sauce over enchiladas and sprinkle with cheese. Bake at 350 degrees for approximately 20 minutes.

Beefy Skillet Pasta
Serves 4

1 lb. Ground beef or 1 pint canned ground beef
2 Cups Spaghetti sauce
¼ Tsp. Salt
¼ Tsp. Black pepper
3 Cups Hot cooked Fusilli, spiral pasta
½ Cup Mozzarella or cheddar cheese, shredded or dried, rehydrated or Parmesan

Cook beef (or reheat) in a large skillet over medium high heat until browned and crumbled. Drain, and return beef to pan. Add pasta sauce, salt, and pepper; cook 2 minutes, stirring occasionally. Add pasta, and cook 2 minutes. Sprinkle with cheese, and cook 1 minute or until cheese melts.

Beef and Black Bean Soup
Serves 4

1 lb. Ground beef or 1 pint canned ground beef
2 Tsp. Mexican seasoning, salt free
2 Cans Black beans, 15 Oz., rinsed and drained
2 Cup Pepper stir fry, frozen, slightly thawed or dried, rehydrated
1 Can Beef stock, 14.5 Oz., low fat, low salt
1 Cup Chunky salsa

Cook beef in a large saucepan over medium high heat until beef is crumbled and cooked through. Drain, and return to pan; stir in seasoning. Mash 1 can of beans with a fork. Add mashed beans and remaining Can of beans into the beef mixture. Stir in peppers and broth; bring to a boil. Reduce heat, and stir in salsa; simmer uncovered for 5 minutes.

Taco Soup
Serves 6

1 lb. Ground beef or 1 pint canned ground beef
2 Cans Tomatoes diced with green chilies mild, 10 Oz.
1 Can Green chilies, diced, 4.5 Oz., drained
1 Can Black beans, 15 Oz., drained and rinsed
1 Can Kidney beans , 15 Oz., rinsed and drained
1 pkg. Taco seasoning, 1.25 Oz.
½ pkg. Original Ranch Salad Dressing Mix
2 Cup Water
2 Cup Corn, frozen or dry, rehydrated

In a large pot, cook beef until done (or heated through), about 5 minutes. Drain any extra grease. Add the tomatoes, green chilies, beans, taco seasoning, ranch dressing mix, water, and corn. Bring to a boil; reduce heat, and cook for 7 to 10 minutes.

Mexican Lasagna
Serves 6

1 lb. Ground beef, or turkey, or chicken or 1 pint canned ground beef
1 Tb. Onion minced, dried
1 Can Tomato sauce, 8 Oz.
1 package Taco seasoning, 1.25 Oz.
4 Oz. Black olives, chopped
3/4 Cup Ricotta cheese or cottage cheese or alfredo sauce
1 Egg yolks
6 Oz. Mozzarella cheese, sliced, or dried grated cheese, rehydrated
8 Flour tortillas, 8 inch, quartered
1 Cup Cheddar cheese, grated, or dry cheese, rehydrated or Parmesan

Brown (or reheat) ground meat in a skillet, and drain. Mix together dried onion, meat, tomato sauce, and taco seasoning with a fork. Add the chopped olives. In a separate bowl, mix together the cheese or alfredo sauce and egg yolk; stir to combine. Layer ⅓ meat mix, ½ mozzarella cheese, ½ ricotta mix, and ½ tortillas; repeat making sure to end with meat mixture. Cook, covered with wax paper, about 8 minutes in microwave. Sprinkle cheddar cheese on top, and cook 2 more minutes on high in microwave. Alternately, you can bake in an oven at 350 for 40 minutes.

Slow Cooked Cincinnati Chili
Serves 6

1 lb. Ground beef or 1 pint canned ground beef
1 Can Tomatoes, 28 Oz. crushed
2 Onions, red, chopped
4 Carrots, sliced
⅓ Cup BBQ sauce
3 Tb. Chili powder
2 Tbs. Vinegar, red wine
2 Tbs. Molasses, light
1 Tb. Paprika
½ Tsp. Allspice, ground
¼ Tsp. Cloves, ground
1 Tb. Cornmeal
¼ Cup Sour cream or powdered sour cream, reconstituted, optional

Brown beef and transfer to a 6 quart slow cooker or large pot, along with tomatoes, onions, carrots, barbecue sauce, chili powder, vinegar, molasses, paprika, allspice, and cloves; mix well. Cover, cooking on low 8 to 10 hours or on high 4 to 5 hours, until vegetables are tender. Or heat covered pot to boiling and place in a wonder oven. About 20 (or 60 for wonder oven) minutes before the cooking time is up, slowly stir in cornmeal. Cook until thickened on high, about 15 minutes. Serve topped with sour cream.

Minestra, Greek Beef and Orzo
Serves 6

1 lb. Ground beef or 1 pint canned ground beef
3 Tb. Onion, minced
1 package Orzo pasta
1 Can Tomato paste, 8 Oz.
¼ Cup Butter, melted
2 Quarts Water
Salt and pepper, to taste

Brown or reheat and crumble ground beef and onion in a saucepan. Put in 4 quart pot and add water and tomato paste. Bring to a boil. Add pasta and reduce to simmer after 5 minutes. Simmer for up to 15 minutes (stir frequently) or until water is almost absorbed. Add melted butter. Season to taste and serve.

Slow Cooked Chili
Serves 8

2 lb. Ground beef or 2 pints of canned ground beef
1 Onion, chopped, or 1 Cup dry, rehydrated
1 Bell pepper, green, chopped or dried, rehydrated
3 Celery rib, chopped or dried, rehydrated
1 Can Tomatoes, 28 Oz.
2 Cans Beans, kidney or pinto
3 Tsp. Chili pepper
1 Tsp. Garlic salt
1 Tsp. Hot pepper sauce
Salt and pepper, to taste

Brown the ground beef, then combine all in the crockpot and cook on low 8, 10 hours or high 4 hours. Or heat to boiling and place in a wonder oven to finish cooking over 3 - 5 hours.

Baked Spaghetti
Serves 8

2 lb. Ground beef or 2 pints canned ground beef
2 Onion, chopped or 1 Cup dry onion, rehydrated
2 Bell pepper, green, chopped or dried and rehydrated
2 Tsp. Garlic, minced
2 Cans Tomato soup
2 Cans Cream of mushroom soup
2 Cans water
1 lb. Cheddar cheese, grated, or dry cheese, rehydrated or Parmesan
1 lb. Spaghetti noodles, cooked

Brown or reheat and crumble meat, onions, pepper, garlic, and a dash of salt and pepper. Mix soups and water on stove until warm. Combine soup mixture with cheese and meat until cheese melts. Add cooked spaghetti. Put into two greased pans, and bake at 350° until bubbly.

Picadillo
Serves 4

1 lb. Ground beef or 1 pint canned ground beef
1 Bell pepper, green, chopped, optional or dry rehydrated
1 Can Salsa style chunky tomatoes, 14.5 Oz.
1 Cup Black beans, rinsed and drained
½ Cup Raisins

Cook or reheat beef and bell peppers in 12 inch nonstick skillet over medium heat for 8 to 10 minutes, stirring occasionally, until beef is brown; drain. Stir in remaining ; reduce heat to low. Cover and simmer 5 to 7 minutes, stirring occasionally, until hot

Spanish Rice with Ground Beef
Serves 8

1 Tsp. Olive oil
1 Onion, chopped, or 1 Cup dry, rehydrated
1 Bell pepper, green, chopped, optional
1 lb. Ground beef, or turkey, or chicken or 1 pint canned ground beef
2 Cup Water
1 ½ Cup Dry white or brown quick cooking rice
1 Can Tomatoes, 28 Oz., whole or crushed
1 Tb. Chili powder
¼ Tsp. Salt
¼ Tsp. Black pepper

In a large pot, heat oil and add the onion, bell pepper and meat and cook until the meat is browned. Add the rest of the ingredients and mix everything well. Bring to a boil, cover and simmer over low heat for 20 to 30 minutes, depending on the cook time for the rice.

Frankfurter Casserole with Sauerkraut
Serves 6

2 lbs. Sauerkraut
2 Cups beer
2 lbs. wieners or other sausages
Dijon mustard

Preheat oven to 350. Drain the sauerkraut and layer in a baking dish. Add beer and bake one hour. Add wieners and bake another 20 minutes.

Hamburger Casserole
Serves 6

2 Tb. Olive Oil
1 Cup rehydrated dry onion diced
1 lb. Ground beef or 1 pint canned ground beef
2 Cups rehydrated dry mushrooms
1 Can crushed tomatoes, 28 oz. (or 2 14.4 oz. cans)
2 Tb. Parsley
1 Tb. sweet paprika
1 tsp. pepper
12 oz. egg noodles
2 Tb. Butter
1 Cup grated cheddar cheese, dry rehydrated
1 Cup grated Parmesan

Heat a pot of salted water to boils the noodles. Meanwhile, heat oil in a skillet and sauté onion. Add beef and stir to break up large clumps. Add tomatoes, parsley, paprika and pepper. Preheat oven to 350°. When noodles are done, toss them with butter to coat. In a baking dish, layer half the noodles, half the sauce, the other half of the noodles, then sauce and top with cheese. Bake until bubbly, about 20 minutes.

Sausage, Red Bean and Potato Casserole
Serves 6

2 Cups red beans, soaked in water overnight
1 Tb. Salt
1 pint canned sausage, crumbled
2 Cups dried apples, rehydrated
1 ½ Cups dried diced onion, rehydrated
½ Cup brown sugar
1 Tb. garlic
¼ C tomato powder in 1 Cup water, or 1 small can tomato sauce
1 tsp. chili powder
½ tsp. black pepper

Place drained beans in a large, oven proof pot and add water to cover. Simmer until done, about 1 to 1 ½ hours. Stir in salt. Preheat oven to 325. In a skillet warm and crumble sausage. Add sausage and remaining ingredients to beans and stir to combine. Put the pot in the over, covered and bake about an hour.

Enchilada Layered Casserole
Serves 6

1 lb. Ground beef or 1 pint canned ground beef
1 Can Enchilada sauce
1 Cup Salsa
12 Corn tortillas
2 Cup Corn, frozen
1 lb. Cheddar cheese, grated, or dry cheese, rehydrated or Parmesan

In a skillet, brown ground beef; drain. Stir in enchilada sauce and salsa; set aside. Place two tortillas, overlapping as necessary, in the bottom of a greased 13 in. x 9 in. x 2 in. baking dish. Cover with one third of the meat mixture; top with 1 cup corn; sprinkle with 1 ⅓ cups cheese. Repeat layers once, then top with remaining tortillas, meat and cheese. Bake, uncovered, at 350° for 30 minutes or until bubbly

Crock Pot Tamale Casserole

Serves 6

1 lb. Ground beef or 1 pint canned ground beef
1 Egg
1 ½ Cup Milk, or dry milk, reconstituted
3/4 Cup Cornmeal
1 Can Corn, whole kernel,
  drained
1 Can Diced tomatoes, 14.5
  Oz., undrained
1 Can Black olives, sliced, drained
1 package Chili seasoning mix
1 Tsp. Seasoned salt
1 Cup Cheddar cheese, grated, or dry cheese, rehydrated or Parmesan

In a skillet, cook beef over medium heat until no longer pink; drain. In a bowl, combine the egg, Milk, or dry milk, reconstituted and cornmeal until smooth. Add corn, tomatoes, olives, chili seasoning, seasoned salt and beef. Transfer to a greased slow cooker. Cover and cook on high for 3 hours and 45 minutes. Sprinkle with cheese; cover and cook 15 minutes longer or until cheese is melted.

Beef Pot Pie with Cheese Crust
Serves 8

2 pints canned beef chunks
1 Onion, chopped or ⅓ Cup dry, rehydrated
1 Cup Carrots, dry, rehydrated
1 ¼ Cup Flour, divided
¼ Cup Butter, margarine or shortening
1 C Beef or chicken stock plus ¼ Cup, divided
1 Tb. Horseradish, creamed - optional
1 Cup Corn, frozen, or dry, rehydrated
2 Cups mushrooms, dry, rehydrated
1 Cup Flour
1 Tsp. Salt
⅓ Cup Shortening
⅓ Cup Cheddar cheese, grated, or dry cheese, rehydrated or Parmesan
2 ½ Tb. Cold water

Cut beef into 1 inch cubes and reserve stock. In a food processor or bowl and whisk, pulse the 1 cup flour, shortening, salt, and cheese. Add water until a dough is formed. In a large stock pot, melt butter and sauté the 1/4 cup of flour for about 5 minutes. Slowly stir in the quart of stock using any reserved from the beef. Stir until thickened. Add mushrooms, horseradish and beef and simmer until heated through. Preheat oven to 375. Rest the crust dough 10 minutes at room temperature then roll out to size to cover baking dish. Pour filling into a baking dish and cover with crust. Crimp edges. Cover loosely with foil and bake 40 minutes.

Cheesy Beef and Corn Casserole
Serves 6

1 lb. Ground beef or 1 pint canned ground beef
½ Onion, chopped or dry, rehydrated
1 Can Tomato soup
1 Can Creamed corn, small can
1 Can Mushrooms, sliced
2 Cup Cheddar cheese, grated, or dry cheese, rehydrated or ¾ Cup Parmesan
1 Can Olives, chopped, small can
2 ½ Cup Noodles

Preheat oven to 400. Prepare noodles according to package directions; drain and set aside. Meanwhile, brown or reheat and crumble ground beef; drain excess fat. Add onions and cook until golden. Add soup, cooked noodles, corn, olives and mushrooms. Simmer 5 minutes. Stir in half of the cheese. Place in a 2 quart casserole dish and top with remaining cheese. Bake at 400° for 20 minutes.

Low and Slow Braised Beef Stew
Serves 6

1 lb. Beef stew meat or 1 pint canned beef
2 Tsp. Salt
3 Celery stalks, or ½ C dried and rehydrated
½ Tsp. Black pepper
1 Onion
1 Tb. Sugar
3 Carrots or 1 Cup sliced dehydrated carrots, rehydrated
2 Tbs. Minute tapioca
3 Potatoes or 2 Cups dehydrated diced potatoes, rehydrated
1 ½ Cup Tomato juice or V8

Preheat oven to 375°. Cover bottom of a heavy pan with meat. Cut and arrange vegetables on top. Combine dry ingredients and sprinkle on top of vegetables. Add tomato juice. Cover pan tightly with foil or lid. Bake four hours. Do not peek or stir.

Tator Tot Casserole
Serves 6

1 lb. Ground beef or 1 pint canned ground beef, browned
1 package Tator tots or hash browns, frozen or dried, rehydrated
1 Can Minestrone Soup, concentrated
1 Can Cream of mushroom soup

Combine browned ground beef and soups in a casserole dish. Put tator tots on top and bake at 375° until tots are crisp and mixture is bubbling. To stretch this recipe you can add cooked pasta such as egg noodles, or shells, and some parmesan cheese to mixture. You can even add canned or dried veggies to the mixture.

Chili Con Carne
Serves 6

1 ½ lb. Ground beef or 1 pint canned ground beef
1 Can Red beans, 15 Oz.
1 Can chili beans
1 Can Kidney beans, 15 Oz.
1 Can Black beans, 15 0z
1 Can Pinto beans, 15 Oz., rinsed and drained
1 Can Stewed tomatoes, 28 Oz.
1 Chili seasoning mix – optional – or 1 Tb chili powder, ½ tsp. cayenne

Brown or reheat and crumble hamburger in large pot, add cans of beans and tomatoes. The juices from the beans make a really nice sauce, but you may add chili seasoning if you want to. Simmer 30 – 60 minutes. Serve with crackers and shredded cheese.

Beef Stroganoff
Serves 4

1 ½ lb. Bottom round steak or 1 pint canned beef chunks
1 Can Cream of mushroom soup
½ Cup Milk, or dry milk, reconstituted
½ Cup Sour cream or sour cream powder reconstituted
1 package Egg noodles, twisted

Cut meat into bite size pieces. Let meat cook to get tender, its best to simmer meat in the soup and Milk, or dry milk, reconstituted for 30 minute to an hour. Add sour cream. Meanwhile, cook noodles according to package directions. Pour sauce over noodles and serve.

Vegetable Beef Soup with Pasta
Serves 6

1 lb. Ground beef or 1 pint canned ground beef
1 Can Green beans, small Can
1 Can Carrots, small can
1 Can Peas, 8 Oz.
1 Can Corn, small can
1 Can Tomato soup
1 Can Stewed tomatoes, 16 Oz.
4 Beef bouillon cubes
8 Potatoes, peeled, quartered or 3 Cups dehydrated, diced potatoes, rehydrated
2 Cup Pasta, cooked

Put everything in a pot and simmer until hamburger, potatoes and pasta are done. Cook until everything is done and heated through, and the flavors have blended. Also you can add any other vegetables that you would like to this recipe.

Shepherd's Pie
Serves 6

1 ½ lb. Ground beef or 1 pint canned ground beef
2 Tbs. Olive oil
1 Cup Onion, chopped or ¼ C dried onion, rehydrated
1 Cup Beef gravy or 1 C bouillon cooked with 1 Tb. Butter and 1 Tb. Flour
Salt and pepper, to taste
2 Cup Instant mashed potatoes, prepared

Preheat oven to 400. In an oven proof skillet, heat oil over medium high and sauté onions until softened. Add beef and cook until done. Add gravy and heat until simmering. Meanwhile prepare potatoes according to package and spoon over beef or pipe over using a piping bag with large star tip. Bake 15 to 20 minutes until lightly browned.

Franks and Beans
Serves 4

1 package Hot dogs, or 1 pint canned wieners
1 Onion, chopped, or 1 Cup dry, rehydrated
2 Tbs. Olive oil
2 Tsp. Dry mustard
1 Can Baked beans, 28 Oz.
½ Cup Ketchup
3 Tb. Brown sugar
Dash Black pepper, to taste
1 Tb. Butter

Sauté franks in oil with onion, butter, mustard and pepper. Add beans, stir in ketchup and sugar. Bake in 8" square pan at 350° for 20 minutes.

Kid Favorite Cheesy Mac and Beef
Serves 8

1 ½ lb. Ground beef, browned or 2 pints canned ground beef
1 Can Stewed tomatoes, 16 Oz., drained
1 Can Spaghetti sauce,   28 Oz.
2 package Macaroni and cheese, cooked
2 Cup Mozzarella cheese, grated, or Parmesan

Preheat oven to 350. Prepare Mac and Cheese according to package directions. Meanwhile, in a skillet over medium heat, brown the ground beef until done; drain. Add tomatoes and spaghetti sauce and pour into a 13 X 9 baking dish. Top with cheese and bake 20 minutes.

Indian Beef and Corn Stew
Serves 4

1 lb. Ground beef or 1 pint canned ground beef
1 Onion, chopped, or 1 Cup dry, rehydrated
1 Bell pepper, green, chopped
2 Cup Corn, fresh or frozen
1 Tsp. Garlic, minced
1 Can Tomatoes, 14.5 Oz. diced
1 Tsp. Seasoned salt

In a large skillet over medium high heat, brown hamburger with onion and pepper. Add remaining , simmer 25 minutes and serve.

Easy Beefy Soup
Serves 10

1 lb. Ground beef or 1 pint canned ground beef
2 Cans Minestrone soup, 10 Oz.
1 Can Beans, ranch style, 16 Oz.
2 Cans Tomatoes, stewed 14.5 Oz.
1 Can Corn, 15 Oz. or 1 Cup dried corn, rehydrated
1 Cup Hash browns, frozen or dried

Brown and drain the ground beef. Meanwhile in a soup pot, start remaining ingredients on medium high, until boiling then reduce heat. Add beef and simmer 15 minutes. Add water to adjust consistency as desired. Adjust seasonings and serve.

Crock Pot Alphabet Soup
Serves 8

1 lb. Beef stew meat or 1 pint canned beef chunks
1 Can Diced tomatoes, 28 Oz.
1 Can Beef stock
3 Cups Water
1 package Onion soup mix
1 ½ Cup Alphabet pasta, uncooked
2 Cups dehydrated mixed vegetables, rehydrated

Combine beef, tomatoes, beef stock, water, vegetables and soup mix in a crock pot. Cook on low for 8 hours. Or bring to a boil in a regular pot with lid and finish cooking in a wonder oven. Add pasta 30 minutes before serving. Combine and serve.

Slow Cooked Beef Lentil Soup
Serves 8

1 lb. Beef stew meat or 1 pint canned beef chunks
3 Carrots, peeled and chopped or dehydrated carrots
3 Potatoes, peeled and diced or 2 cups dehydrated diced potatoes
1 Onion, chopped, or 1 Cup dry, rehydrated
3 Celery rib, chopped, optional
2 Cans Tomatoes, chopped
2 Cans Beef stock
½ lb. Lentils
½ Tsp. Marjoram, dried
2 Tsp. Seasoned salt

Layer lentils, vegetables and meat in slow cooker and pour stock over. Add seasonings. Cook on low for 9, 10 hours. Or bring to a boil in a pot with lid and finish cooking in a wonder oven.

Meatball Hoagies
Serves 4

4 Hoagie sandwich rolls
1 lb. Meatballs, cooked, from canned
1 Cup Spaghetti sauce
¼ lb. Provolone cheese, sliced or dry cheese, rehydrated

Preheat oven to 400°. Reheat the Meatballs for heated through; add sauce. Heat the spaghetti sauce over medium high heat covered, stirring occasionally. Split hoagies, place on cooking sheet and toast in the oven 5 minutes. Top with Meatball and sauce mixture and cheese. Return to oven until cheese melts.

Carne Asada Tacos
Serves 8

3 lb. Beef chuck or skirt steak or 2 pints canned beef chunks
⅓ Cup Lime juice
1 Onion, chopped, or 1 Cup dry, rehydrated
3 Tb. Garlic powder
1 Tb. Oregano, dried
2 Tbs. Seasoned salt
2 Tb. Oil
1 dozen Tortillas, warmed
Taco condiments; hot sauce, cheese, onions, cilantro

In a bowl, combine lime juice, onion, garlic powder, oregano and season salt. Add beef and stir to coat. Heat a skillet with cooking oil over medium heat. Add meat and stir to heat through. Serve with hot tortillas and taco condiments: grated cheese, diced onion, cilantro, and sour cream.

Tip:

Ground beef is so easy to can and just wonderful to have on hand for quick meals. Remember to drain the fat before canning to get the best seals. Many people enjoy great success by boiling their beef for canning, because it stays separate and tender.

Chicken and Turkey

Chicken Pasta with Cheese and Caramelized Onions
Serves 8

2 Cups Chicken, cooked, chopped or 2 pints canned chicken
1 lb. Pasta, bite size, fresh or dried
1 Onion, chopped, or 1 Cup dry, rehydrated
4 Tsp. Garlic, minced
¼ Cup Olive oil, divided
1 Cup Blue cheese, crumbled or Parmesan
4 Tb. Pine nuts, toasted

Bring a large pot of salted water to boil covered and cook pasta according to package directions. Combine 3 Tb. of the oil and onion in a skillet and sauté until lightly golden, 10 – 15 minutes, stirring periodically. Add remaining olive oil. Add garlic and chicken to onion mixture and cook until heated through. Add cooked pasta and cheese; toss to combine. Top with pine nuts and serve.

Chicken Divan
Serves 4

3 Cups broccoli, fresh or dried
4 Tb. Butter or Margarine
¼ Cup Flour
2 Cups Chicken stock or bouillon and water equivalent
1 can evaporated milk, 5 oz.
1 tsp. lemon juice
½ tsp. salt
¼ tsp. pepper
¼ tsp. Curry powder
2 pints canned chicken, sliced
½ Cup Parmesan cheese, grated

Preheat oven to 350°. In a pot of salted water, cook or reconstitute broccoli until tender, drain and reserve. In a sauce pan over medium heat, cook butter and flour, stirring for about 2 minutes. Add chicken stock and evaporated milk, stirring until thickened. Remove from heat and add lemon juice, salt, pepper and curry powder. Stir to combine. Layer chicken in the bottom of a baking dish. Cover with half the sauce. Add the broccoli, and then add ¼ cup of the Parmesan cheese to the sauce and stir. Layer the remaining sauce over the broccoli, and then sprinkle on the remaining ¼ cup of Parmesan. Bake until bubbly and golden, about 30 minutes.

Chicken and Wild Rice Soup

Serves 8

1 pint canned chicken, chopped
1 package Long Grain Wild Rice Mix
2 Cans Cream of chicken Soup
1 Can Cream of Mushroom Soup
4 Cups boiling water

Cook rice according to package directions. Add remaining ingredients and simmer until heated through. Adjust the consistency by adding more if needed.

Chicken with Olives, Lemon and Capers

Serves 4

1 pint canned chicken
1 Can Tomatoes, diced, 14.5 Oz.
2/3 Cups Olives (black or green), small
4 Tsp. Lemon zest
¼ Cup Capers salted, rinsed and chopped
2 Tb. Cup Olive oil
Salt and pepper, to taste

Combine tomatoes, olives, zest, capers, oil and seasonings in a skillet over medium high heat. Add chicken and heat, stirring until heated through. This dish is great over some rice or potatoes to sop up the sauce.

Chicken and Dumplings
Serves 8

2 pints canned chicken
2 Cans Chicken broth, or 4 Cups chicken bouillon
½ Cup Carrots, dry and rehydrated
½ Cup Onion, diced, dry and rehydrated
½ Cup Peas, dry and rehydrated
4 Cups Flour
1 ½ tsp. Salt
½ Cup shortening
1 ½ cup Water

In a bowl, whisk together flour, salt and shortening until the size of small peas. Add water a little at a time, stirring until a stiff dough forms. Pat out on and then roll to ¼" thickness. Cut into squares.

In a pot with a well-fitting lid, bring chicken stock to a boil. Add chicken and vegetables. Drop in dumplings one at a time. Cover and simmer 30 – 45 minutes until dumplings are done.

Spiced Turkey with Rice Pilaf and Lima Beans
Serves 4

1 tsp. turmeric
½ tsp. allspice
2 ½ tsp. salt
½ tsp. pepper
¼ tsp. ground cloves
1 Pint canned turkey
4 Tb. Butter or margarine
½ Cup diced carrots, canned or dry and rehydrated
1 Cup long grain rice, rinsed in water and drained
1 ½ Cups water
½ Cup Lima beans, fresh or canned

Preheat oven to 350. In a bowl, mix together turkey and spices. In a stove and oven safe pot with lid melt butter over medium high heat. Add carrots and rice and stir for two minutes. Add turkey, water, salt and pepper. Bring to a simmer and then cover and bake 20 minutes. Let rest 20 minutes, then fluff and serve.

Slow Cooked Green Turkey Chili
Serves 4

1 pint canned turkey, chopped
1 Onion, chopped, or ½ Cup dry, rehydrated
1 Can Cannellini beans, 15 Oz., rinsed and drained
1 Cut Corn, dry rehydrated or canned (8 oz.)
1 Cup Green tomatillo salsa
1 Can Chopped green chili peppers, 4.5 Oz.
2 Tsp. Garlic, minced
1 ½ Tsp. Cumin, ground
½ Tsp. Salt
⅓ Cup Cilantro leaves, chopped for garnish, optional or 1 TB dried cilantro
To serve: sour cream, or dry, rehydrated

Place turkey, onion, beans and corn in a crock pot or pot. Combine salsa, chilies, garlic, cumin, and salt then pour over ingredients in crock, pot or Dutch Oven. Cover and simmer about an 45 minutes or place in a wonder oven for a longer. Cut turkey into bite sized pieces (if needed) then return to pot. Stir in cilantro, if using. Serve with condiments.

Lemon Chicken Soup

Serves 4

1 quart chicken stock
1 Can cream of chicken soup
1 Cup rice, uncooked
1 pint canned chicken with broth
¼ Cup lemon juice
4 Slices dehydrated Lemon
1/3 Cup carrots, dry and rehydrated

In a large pot, add all ingredients. Bring to a boil, reduce to simmer and cook 15 – 20 minutes or until the rice is tender.

Chicken and Potato Pizzaiola

Serves 4

1 pint canned chicken, cubed
4 Cups dry sliced potatoes, rehydrated
2 Cans Diced tomatoes, drained
6 Tb. Olive oil
2 Tb Oregano
Salt and pepper
½ Cup Parmesan cheese, divided

Preheat the oven to 400. Reserving ¼ cup of Parmesan, combine all ingredients in a 9 x 12 dish. Top with remaining Parmesan and bake about 35 minutes until potatoes are tender.

Slow Cooked Chicken and Bean Stew
Serves 2

1 lb. Chicken thighs, boneless skinless, halved or 1 pint canned chicken
1 Onion, chopped, or 1 Cup dry, rehydrated
1 Can Tomatoes, diced with peppers, celery and onions– 14.5 Oz., drained
3/4 Cup Broth
1/8 Tsp. Cayenne pepper, ground
¼ Tsp. Salt
¼ Tsp. Pepper
3/4 Cup Corn, frozen or dried
3/4 Cup Lima beans, frozen or dried
1 Tb. Dijon mustard
¼ Tsp. Salt
¼ Tsp. Pepper

Combine in crock: chicken onion, tomatoes, broth, cayenne, salt and pepper, corn and lima beans. Cover and cook on high for 3 hours or low for 5 hours or use a regular pot with lid, heat to boiling and then place in a wonder oven to finish cooking over a few hours. Cut chicken into 1 inch pieces. Return to pot along with mustard, and remaining salt and pepper. Cook 20 minutes more and then serve. Great with mashed potatoes.

Chicken Casserole
Serves 8

8 Slices of day old bread, torn
½ Tsp. Sage
2 Pints canned chicken
½ Cups dry celery, reconstituted
½ Cup Mayonnaise
¼ Cup dry Onion dices, rehydrated
Salt and pepper
2 eggs or equivalent rehydrated egg powder
2 Cups of milk reconstituted from dry milk

For the sauce:
2 Tb. Butter, margarine or shortening
2 Tb. Flour
1 Cup chicken stock or bouillon with water to make 1 Cup
2/3 Cup milk reconstituted from powder
1 small can evaporated milk – 5 oz.
Salt and pepper

2 Cups grated dried cheese, rehydrated or Parmesan

Layer bread in the bottom of a large baking dish. Mix together chicken, celery, mayonnaise and onion and spread over bread. Mix together eggs and milk and pour over bread and chicken mixture. Let sit 2 hours, refrigerated or up to overnight.
Preheat oven to 350. In a saucepan, melt butter and stir in flour. Cook two minutes and add both milks. Cook and stir until thickened. Season with salt and pepper. Pour over baking dish. Top with cheese and bake until bubbly and golden – about 40 minutes.

Chicken and Rice
Serves 4

4 Chicken breasts, boneless skinless, 5 Oz. each or 1 pint canned chicken
1 Tb. Olive oil
1 Can Cream of chicken soup
1 ½ Cups Water
¼ Tsp. Paprika
¼ Tsp. Pepper
1 ½ Cup Instant brown rice, uncooked
2 Cup Broccoli flowerets, fresh, frozen or dried, rehydrated

Brown or reheat chicken in oil over med high heat; set aside. Using the same skillet combine soup, water, paprika, and pepper and bring to a boil. Add rice and broccoli. Reduce heat. Add chicken. Cover and cook 5 minutes until chicken and rice are completely cooked.

Chicken Broccoli Casserole
Serves 8

2 Pints canned chicken
½ Cup rehydrated dry celery
½ Cup rehydrated dry carrots
½ Cup rehydrated dry diced onion
3 Cups dry Broccoli florets, rehydrated

6 Tb. Butter, margarine or shortening
1 Cup breadcrumbs
¼ Cup flour
1 Cup milk, reconstituted from powder
Salt and pepper
1 Cup Mayonnaise
2 tsp. Lemon juice

Preheat the oven to 350. Layer the vegetable in the bottom of a baking dish. In a saucepan melt butter. In a bowl, pour half the melted butter over the breadcrumbs and stir to combine. Add flour to the remaining butter and cook, stirring 2 minutes. Add milk and cook, stirring until thickened, about 12 minutes. Remove from heat and season with salt and pepper. Stir in mayonnaise and lemon juice. Pour over vegetables and top with buttered breadcrumbs. Bake 35 minutes or until golden and bubbly.

Chicken Noodle Mushroom Casserole
Serves 6

12 oz. egg noodles
4 Tb butter, margarine or shortening divided
1 pint canned chicken, diced, broth reserved
2 Cups dry mushrooms, reconstituted
¼ Cup dry diced onion, rehydrated
¼ Cup flour
Additional chicken broth or bouillon to make 1 Cup total
1 tsp. Rosemary, dried and crumbled

Preheat oven to 350. Boil noodles in salted water until just done, drain and toss with 2 Tb. of the butter, layer in a baking dish, top with chicken, and set aside. In a skillet, heat the remaining 2 Tb butter and sauté the mushrooms and onion together. Add the flour and stir together, cooking about 2 minutes. Add the chicken broth and cook, stirring, until thickened. Stir in the rosemary and pour the mixture in the baking dish. Bake until bubbly and golden.

White Chili
Serves 4

1 lb. Chicken, cooked, diced or 1 pint canned chicken, diced
1 Onion, diced or ½ Cup dry onion, rehydrated
2 Tsp Garlic, minced
1 Can Great Northern beans, 15 Oz.
1 Can Garbanzo beans 16 Oz.
2 ½ Cup Chicken broth
1 Green chilies, diced 4 Oz.
2 Tsp. Chili powder
½ Tsp. Cumin, ground
Dash Cayenne pepper, ground

Sauté onion and garlic in bottom of soup pot. Add remaining ingredients and simmer 20 – 30 minutes until cooked or heated through.

Chicken Chili
Serves 4

1 lb. Chicken, cooked, diced or 1 pint canned chicken
1 Onion, diced, or ½ Cup dry onion, rehydrated
2 Tsp. Garlic, minced
1 Tb. Oil
1 Can Black beans
1 Can Kidney beans
2 ½ Cup Salsa (or diced tomatoes)
1 Can Green chili, diced 4 Oz.
2 Tsp. Chili powder
½ Tsp. Cumin, ground

Sauté onion and garlic in bottom of soup pot. Add remaining ingredients and simmer 20 minutes.

Teriyaki Turkey Breast with Pineapple
Serves 4

1 Tb. Olive oil
1 lb. Turkey breast, boneless skinless, cut crosswise into ½ inch thick strips, or 1 pint canned turkey, cut into large chunks
Salt and pepper, to taste
1 Pineapple chunks in juice, 20 Oz. canned
1 Cup Pickled onions, drained
⅔ Cup Teriyaki sauce
¼ Cup Honey

Over medium heat in a large skillet, heat oil. Season entire turkey breast with salt and pepper and put in hot pan. Lightly sear until golden brown on both sides about 2 minutes on each side.
Add the pineapple, including juice, onions, teriyaki and honey and bring to a simmer. Cover the pan partially and simmer for about 5 minutes until the turkey is cooked through.

Arrange turkey on platter, spoon sauce over top, and serve.

Turkey (or Chicken) and Dumplings
Serves 6

3 Cups Cooked turkey, chopped or 2 pints canned turkey or chicken
2 Tbs. Butter
2 Celery stalks, chopped or dry celery reconstituted
8 Oz. Mushrooms, sliced or dry mushrooms rehydrated
1 Cup Onions, chopped or ½ cup dry onion, rehydrated
1 Tsp. Garlic, minced
2 Cup Peas and carrots, frozen or dry, rehydrated
1 Can Chicken broth, 14 Oz.
2 Packets of turkey gravy mix
1 ½ Cup Biscuit mix
3/4 Cup Sour cream
1 Tsp. Sage, dried
1 Tsp. Pepper, fresh ground

Melt butter in Dutch oven over medium heat. Add celery, mushrooms, onion and garlic cooking for 2 minutes.
Add turkey, peas, carrots, broth, and turkey gravy. Bring to boil over med high heat. For dumplings combine baking mix, sour cream, sage and pepper. Drop heaping spoonfuls of dumplings into hot soup. Boil uncovered for 10 minutes. Cover and cook 10 minutes more. Dumplings are done when dry in center. Serve immediately.

Lemon, Dijon, Rosemary Rubbed Chicken
Serves 4

1 pint canned chicken
1 Tb. Lemon juice
1 Tb. Olive oil
1 Tb. Dijon mustard
1 Tb. Garlic, minced
1 Tb. Rosemary, fresh, chopped
½ Tsp. Salt
½ Tsp. Pepper

Combine oil and seasonings, whisk together and add chicken to coat. Soak 30 minutes, then reheat chicken in a skillet over medium heat until warmed through. Serve with rice or buttered noodles.

Chili Rubbed Chicken
Serves 4

1 pint canned chicken
2 Tb. olive oil
1 Tb. Chili powder
1 ½ tsp. Salt
1 Tsp. Garlic powder
½ Tsp. Pepper
¼ Tsp. Cayenne pepper, ground

Combine oil and seasonings, whisk together and add chicken to coat. Marinate 10 minutes, then reheat chicken in a skillet over medium heat until warmed through. Serve with rice or buttered noodles.

Yogurt Marinated Chicken

Serves 4

1 ½ lb. Chicken breasts, boneless skinless or 1 pint canned chicken
6 Oz. Yogurt, plain
1 Tb. Lemon juice
1 ¼ Tsp. Sugar
½ Tsp. Salt
1 Tsp. Paprika
½ Tsp. Coriander, ground
¼ Tsp. Curry powder

Combine in large baking dish. Refrigerate at least one hour; turning at least once. Sauté, broil or grill until chicken is done or heated through.

Rosemary Chicken

Serves 4

6 Chicken breasts, boneless, skinless or 1 pint canned chicken
¼ Cup Olive oil
2 Tsp. Garlic, minced
1 tsp. dry rosemary, crumbled
1 Tb. Balsamic vinegar
Salt and pepper to taste

Combine all ingredients (except chicken). Brush marinade over chicken and let rest 10 minutes. Add chicken and marinade to a skillet and cook over medium heat until heated through. Delicious served over rice.

Slow Cooked Posole
Serves 8

2 Cup Golden hominy, 14.5 Oz.
1 Can Green chili peppers, chopped, 4 Oz.
½ Cup Onion, chopped or ¼ Cup dry onion, rehydrated
2 Tsp. Garlic, minced
1 lb. Chicken breasts, boneless skinless or 1 pint canned chicken, chopped
1 Can Tomatoes, 14.5 Oz., undrained and cut up
2 Cans Chicken broth, 14.5 Oz.
1 Tsp. Oregano, dried
½ Tsp. Cumin, ground
2 Tbs. Cilantro, or 1 tsp. dry cilantro, optional
Optional: Sour cream or sour cream powder, reconstituted

Combine ingredients in 4 quart Slow Cooker, Dutch oven or pot: hominy, chili peppers, onion, garlic, chicken tomatoes, chicken broth, oregano and cumin. Cook on low 5 hours or high 2.5 hours. Or heat to boiling and place in a wonder oven for several hours. Stir in cilantro if using. Garnish with sour cream if desired.

Lemon Garlic Marinated Chicken

Serves 4

1 ½ lb. Chicken or 1 pint canned chicken.
½ Cup Lemon juice
2 Tbs. Garlic, minced
2 Tsp. Oregano, dried
½ Tsp. Salt
1 Tsp. Pepper, fresh ground
½ Cup Olive oil

Combine marinade whisking in olive oil last. Pour over chicken in shallow pan. Refrigerate at least one hour; turning at least once. Sauté, broil or grill until chicken tests done or for canned chicken is heated through.

Chicken Tortilla Soup

Serves 6

2 Cans Diced tomatoes and green chilies, 10 Oz.
2 Cans Chicken broth, 14 Oz.
1 Can Refried beans, 15 Oz.
½ Cup Corn, whole kernel, frozen or dehydrated
2 Cup Chicken, cooked, shredded or 1 pint canned chicken
Corn chips
Monterey jack cheese, shredded or Parmesan

Combine tomatoes and broth. Add beans and corn. Simmer 5 minutes; stirring often. Add chicken. Top with chips and cheese.

Quick Chicken Piccata
Serves 4

1 pint canned chicken, sliced, juiced reserved
¼ Tsp. Salt
¼ Tsp. Pepper, fresh ground
2 Tbs. Butter
1 Shallot, minced or 1 Tb. onion, dry, rehydrated
½ Cup White wine or chicken stock
⅓ Cup Lemon juice
2 Tbs. Capers, chopped
2 Tbs. Parsley, fresh or 1 Tb. dried

Season chicken with salt and pepper. Melt butter in skillet over med high. Cook chicken until warmed through and set aside. Add shallots (or onion) and cook 1 minute. Add wine, lemon and chicken juice and capers. Heat to simmer. Return chicken to pan, spooning sauce over top. Stir in parsley and serve. Delicious over hot, buttered noodles.

Chicken Enchiladas

Serves 6

1 Pint Canned chicken, diced
1 Dan Diced green chilies, 4 oz.
¼ Cup Dry Onion, Chopped, rehydrated
2 Cup Jack cheese, rehydrated, divided
1 Can Green Enchilada Sauce, 19 oz.
1 Can Cream of mushroom soup (or cream of chicken)
Cooking spray
4 Tb. Olive Oil
12 Corn Tortillas

Preheat oven to 350°.

Filling: Mix together chicken, chilies, onion and 1 cup of the cheese. Set aside.

Sauce: Mix together enchilada sauce and soup.

Assembly: Spray a baking dish with cooking spray (or oil) and spread ¼ cup of sauce in the pan. In a medium skillet heat 1 Tb of oil, and soften tortillas one at a time, and then fill with ¼ chicken mixture and place seam side down in the baking dish. Repeat with all the tortillas adding more oil to the skillet as needed. Pour the remaining sauce over the enchiladas, sprinkle on the remaining cheese and bake until hot and bubbly, about 35 minutes.

Chicken with Apple Walnut Chutney
Serves 4

4 Chicken breasts, boneless skinless, 5 Oz. each, cut into chunks
½ Tsp. Ginger, ground
1 Tb. Olive oil
½ Cup Dried tart cherries
1 Apple, large, skin on, sliced into rounds
⅓ Cup Walnuts, coarsely chopped
4 Tsp. Brown sugar
3 Tb. Cider vinegar
Salt and pepper, to taste
¼ Cup Water

Season chicken with salt, pepper and half of the ginger.
Heat oil to medium heat and cook chicken 12 minutes (for raw chicken or just until hot for canned chicken). Set aside. Add fruit and nuts to skillet cooking 2 minutes. Combine brown sugar, water, vinegar, and remaining ginger. Add to fruit and cook 30 seconds. Drizzle chicken and fruit with sauce and serve

Pesto Parmesan Chicken Pasta
Serves 4

1 pint canned chicken
1 package Angel hair pasta, 9 Oz.
4 Carrots, sliced thin, or dehydrated carrots, rehydrated
2 Tbs. Butter
¼ Cup Pesto, or 2 TB olive oil, 1 TB dried basil and 1 tsp. garlic
¼ Cup Parmesan cheese, grated
Olive oil, to taste
Basil, to taste

Boil pasta in salted water until al dente; drain. Return to pot and stir in half of the butter. Cook carrots in skillet over medium heat in remaining butter. Add chicken cooking 3 minutes or until warmed through. Add pesto. Serve chicken atop pasta. Sprinkle with Parmesan, pepper, and basil. Finish with a drizzle of olive oil.

Maple Chicken
Serves 4

1 pint canned chicken
2 Tsp. Steak seasoning blend
2 Tbs. Butter
¼ Cup Maple syrup
¼ Cup Onions, diced or 1 Tb. dry rehydrated diced onion

Heat butter in skillet over med high heat, add onion and sweat slightly. Coat chicken with seasoning; cook until heated through. Cover and set aside. Stir maple syrup into skillet, and cook 2 minutes. Divide chicken among serving plates. Drizzle with syrup mix and serve.

Chicken on Crispy Potatoes
Serves 4

4 Chicken breast fillets or 1 pint canned chicken
Salt and pepper, to taste
3 Cups dehydrated, grated potato (hash browns), soaked and squeezed dry
2 Tbs. Oil
1 Tsp. Garlic, minced, or dry, rehydrated
½ Cup Parmesan cheese, grated

Preheat oven to 425°. Toss potato strips with oil, garlic, Parmesan and pepper. Place on tray lined with baking paper; bake 15 minutes or cook in a skillet until crisp.
Rub salt and pepper into skin of chicken. Fry over high heat skin side down 4 minutes. Turn and cook 1 minute more (or for canned chicken, heat until warm).

Place chicken on the potato rosti and bake 5 minutes more or until hot. Serve when chicken is cooked through and rosti is crisp.

Baked Chicken and Pea Risotto
Serves 4

1 pint canned chicken
2 Cup Arborio or carnaroli rice
2 Tbs. Olive oil
1 Onion, chopped, or ½ Cup dry, rehydrated
1 Tb. Lemon zest
5 Cup Stock
1 ½ Cup Peas, frozen or dehydrated and rehydrated
2 Tbs. Lemon juice
½ Cup Parmesan cheese, grated
Salt and pepper, to taste

Preheat oven to 400°. Heat frying pan over high heat; add oil, onion and zest to the pan and cook 5 minutes. Place onion, rice and stock in baking dish. Cover and bake 20 minutes. Add chicken and peas to the rice, cover and bake 10 minutes more. Stir in lemon juice, Parmesan, salt and pepper. Stir to thicken; serve.

Creamy Chicken and Mushroom Soup
Serves 8

6 Tb. butter, margarine or shortening
1 Cup dry diced onion, rehydrated
3 Tb. Flour
2 tsp. Salt
1 tsp. Pepper
6 cups chicken broth, or chicken bouillon
1 ½ Cups dry mushrooms, sliced, reconstituted
¾ Cup rehydrated dry celery
¾ Cup rehydrated dry carrots
2 Cups rehydrated dry chopped potatoes
1 ½ Cups rehydrated dry corn kernels, thawed
2 tsp. thyme
1 Can evaporated milk, 14.5 oz
¾ cup grated Parmesan, plus more for garnish if desired
1 pint canned chicken with broth

In a large pot, melt the butter over medium heat. Add the onion and sauté until tender, about 6 minutes. Stir in the flour, salt, and pepper and mix until smooth. Add the broth, then bring the soup to a boil. Add the mushrooms, celery, carrots, potatoes, squash, corn, and thyme. Reduce the heat and simmer the soup, covered, until the vegetables are tender, about 20 minutes.

Add the evaporated milk, Parmesan, and chicken. Heat the soup for an additional 10 minutes, but do not let it boil. To serve, ladle the soup into a bowl and sprinkle it with more Parmesan, if desired.

Chicken with Capers and Sun Dried Tomatoes
Serves 4

1 pint canned chicken
1 ½ Tb. Olive oil
½ Cup Chicken broth, or equivalent bouillon
2 Tbs. Lemon juice
½ Cup Sun dried tomatoes, re-hydrated and chopped
2 Tbs. Capers
2 Tb Butter
2 Tbs. Parsley, flat leaf, chopped, or 1 Tb. dried
Salt and pepper to taste

Heat olive oil in frying pan over high heat. Season chicken to taste. Sauté until heated through. Set aside and keep warm. Add broth and tomatoes to pan and cook until reduced by half. Add lemon juice and capers. Pour over chicken, sprinkle with parsley and serve.

Italian Chicken Soup with Dumplings
Serves 8

1/3 Cup breadcrumbs
2 Eggs, beaten or dry equivalent, reconstituted
1 Cup Parmesan cheese
1 pinch of nutmeg
Salt and pepper
2 quarts chicken stock
2 pints home canned chicken
1 Tb dry parsley

Combine breadcrumbs, eggs, cheese, nutmeg, salt and pepper, chill 15 minutes. . In a pot, heat stock until simmering.. Add chicken and parsley. Roll the breadcrumb mixture into balls the size of grapes, and add them all to the simmering soup. Cook about 4 minutes or until dumplings are cooked through (taste one).

Lemon Chicken Pasta
Serves 4

1 package Linguine, 14 Oz.
3 Tb. Olive oil
3 Tb. Capers, salted, rinsed
2 Tsp. Garlic, minced
2 Red chilies, small, seeded and chopped
1 pint canned chicken, shredded
1 Tb. Lemon zest, or 3 slices of dehydrated lemon
1 Cup Basil, fresh, chopped or 2 Tb dry basil
Salt and pepper to taste
½ Cup Parmesan cheese
3 Tb. Lemon juice

Boil pasta in lightly salted water until al dente; drain. Heat a frying pan over high heat. Add oil, capers, garlic and chilies; cook one minute. Add chicken and lemon zest; cook, stirring, 4 minutes. Add pasta, lemon juice, basil and seasonings. Toss; top with Parmesan and serve.

Curried Chicken, Broccoli, and Penne Pasta Bake
Serves 4

1 lb. Penne pasta, mini
1 lb. Broccoli florets, fresh, frozen or dried and rehydrated
1 Cup Onions, chopped or ½ Cup dry, rehydrated
2 Tbs. Olive oil
1 Tsp. Curry powder
1 Tsp. Thyme, dried
½ Tsp. Black Pepper
2 Cups Cooked chicken breast strips, or 1 pint canned chicken, sliced
2 Cups Alfredo pasta sauce, jarred
½ Cup Parmesan cheese, grated
1 Cup Reserved broccoli cooking water

Boil a large pot of water. Cook pasta for half the package cooking time. Add the Broccoli during the last few minutes of cooking. Drain pasta and broccoli. Set aside. Meanwhile, preheat oven to 375 F. Coat a 13 x 9 baking dish with cooking spray. In a small pot, combine the onion, oil, curry powder, thyme, and pepper and cook, stirring, about 5 minutes. Add the spice mixture into the prepared baking dish. Add the chicken, alfredo sauce, Parmesan, pasta, broccoli, and the reserved cooking water to the baking dish. Mix completely. Cover with aluminum foil. Bake for 30 minutes. Remove the foil. Bake for about 20 minutes longer, or until golden and bubbling.

Light Chicken Penne with Tomato Cream Sauce
Serves 4

½ lb. Penne pasta
1 pint canned chicken
2 Tsp. Vegetable oil
1 Cup Evaporated Milk, or dry milk, reconstituted
1 Cup Chicken stock
3/4 Cup Sundried tomatoes, soaked in water and chopped
3 Tb. Parmesan cheese, grated, divided
1 Tb. Tomato paste
2 Tsp. Olive oil
2 Tsp. Garlic, minced
¼ Cup Basil, fresh, chopped, optional

Start a pot of water to boil for the pasta. When ready, cook the pasta until al dente, then drain. Meanwhile preheat a skillet over medium heat with vegetable oil. Cut the chicken into 1 inch pieces. Cook until just heated through. Meanwhile, in a blender, (or bowl with whisk) combine the evaporated milk, stock, tomatoes, tomato paste, olive oil, garlic, and 2 Tbs. of the parmesan cheese. Whir until well blended. When the pasta is done and drained, return it to the pot; add the sauce, and chicken, and stir to combine. Serve the pasta garnished with chopped basil and the remaining Parmesan cheese.

Lemon Chicken Thighs with Orzo and Olives
Serves 4

1 Tb. Olive oil
2/3 Cups Orzo pasta
1 Can Chicken stock
½ Lemon, sliced
1 Tb. Lemon juice
1 Tsp. Oregano, dried
¼ Cup Kalamata olives, drained
1 pint canned chicken

Preheat the oven to 400°. In a Dutch oven or large oven proof skillet with lid, over medium high heat add all the ingredients except the chicken, cover, and bake in the oven until the orzo is tender, about 35 minutes. Add chicken and bake 5 more minutes until heated through.

Chicken Thighs with Mushrooms and Bacon
Serves 4

4 Chicken thighs, bone in with skin or 1 pint canned chicken thighs
2 Bacon slices
2 Cups Mushrooms, sliced, fresh, frozen, canned or dry, rehydrated
1 Can Chicken stock, 14.5 Oz.
1 Tb. Flour
1 Tb. Lemon juice
¼ Cup Parsley, flat leaf, chopped, optional

In a large skillet over medium high heat, cook bacon until crisp. Drain on paper towels. Cook the chicken thighs skin side down, until nicely crisp and golden. Turn over, and cook on the other side until nearly done, about 10 minutes total or for canned chicken, until heated through. Remove the chicken to a bowl, and keep warm. Cook the mushrooms in the pan, adding a Tb. of oil or butter if needed. In a small bowl, whisk together the flour and lemon and some of the stock until smooth. Remove the mushrooms, and add them to the bowl with the chicken.

Add the chicken stock and flour mixture to the pan; stir until well blended, scraping up any browned bits. Add half the parsley, and return the chicken and mushrooms to the pan. Simmer until the sauce thickens and chicken is cooked through, about 8 minutes. Crumble the bacon, and sprinkle over the chicken. Serve garnished with remaining parsley.

Chicken Pot Pie
Serves 6

Pie crust:
>2 cups flour
>¾ cup shortening
>1 teaspoon salt
>1 Tablespoon sugar
>1 egg yolk
>¼ cup cold milk
>1 TB vinegar

For pie crust, combine dry ingredients together. Cut in shortening to pea-size chunks. Mix yolk, milk and vinegar together. Add to dry ingredients and gently mix together. Cover with plastic wrap and chill.

Filling:
>2 ½ Cups chicken stock, or bouillon and water
>¾ Cup butter, margarine or shortening
>⅓ Cup dry onion, rehydrated
>1 Cup dry carrot, rehydrated
>⅓ Cup dry celery, rehydrated
>¾ cup dry green peas, rehydrated
>½ Cup flour
>1 ½ cups milk, or dry milk reconstituted
>2 pints canned chicken, chopped
>½ Tsp. dried thyme
>1 Tb. dry parsley
>2 tsp. salt
>½ tsp. black pepper
>1 pie plate or 6 10-ounce ramekins

Preheat oven to 400°F . In a large skillet, melt butter on medium heat. Add the vegetables, and cook until the onions are tender, about 10 minutes. Add the flour and cook, stirring, one minute more. Whisk in chicken stock and milk. Reduce heat and simmer for 10 minutes, stirring often. Add the chicken meat, thyme, parsley, salt and pepper and stir well.

Divide crust dough in half and roll out dough on a lightly flour surface to a little less than a quarter-inch thick. Cut into 6 rounds to fit ramekins or 2 rounds for pie dish. If using a pie dish, layer one pie crust in the bottom. Add filling to ramekins or pie dish. Add pie crust on top and press to seal. Cut a 1-inch slit in pie top(s). Bake pies for 25 – 35 minutes, or until the pastry is golden and the filling is bubbling. Let stand, for 5-10 minutes before serving.

Tip:

The pie crust recipe above makes wonderful desserts too. Try a rustic pie – roll out a large pie crust and transfer it to a baking sheet. Mound the center with fruit, sugar, and cinnamon leaving about a 4 to 5 inch border clear. Fold the border up over the fruit and bake and 350 for about 30 minutes until the crust is golden and the filling is bubbling.

Red Beans and Rice - 115 -

Grains - 117 -

Mexican Polenta Pie - 117 -
Minnesota Wild Rice Soup - 118 -
Baked Cheesy Grits - 119 -
Barley Mushroom Casserole - 120 -
Baked Polenta - 121 -
Rice, Barley, Lentil and Mushroom Pilaf - 121 -
Cheesy Corn Bread - 122 -
Bulgur and Tomato Salad - 123 -
Baked Rice Pilaf with Carrots - 124 -
Wild Mushroom Risotto with Shrimp and Peas - 124 -

Ham - 125 -

Grilled Cheese With Apple And Ham - 125 -
Ham and Rice Casserole - 125 -
Twice Baked Potatoes with Ham - 126 -
Ham and Asian Noodles - 127 -
Ham and Broccoli Casserole - 128 -
Ham and Noodles Casserole - 129 -
Baked Ham Risotto - 130 -
Baked Ham Carbonara - 131 -
Crispy Ham and Rice Omelet - 131 -
Creamy Ham and Potato Soup - 132 -

Seafood, Shrimp - 133 -

Baked Creole Shrimp - 133 -
Mediterranean Shrimp with Couscous - 134 -
Spiced Garlic Shrimp - 134 -
Shrimp with Rosemary Cannellini Beans - 135 -

Ambrosia Salad - 151 -
Russian Potato Salad - 151 -
Groundnut (Peanut) Soup - 152 -
Corn and Potato Chowder - 153 -

<u>Pasta - 154 -</u>

Penne all'amatriciana - 155 -
Tortellini and Black Bean Soup - 156 -
Tortellini with Mushroom Sauce - 157 -
Tortellini Vegetable Soup - 158 -
Stovetop Mac and Cheese - 158 -
Spaghetti Pie - 159 -
Spaghetti with Clams - 159 -
Sesame Noodles and Peas - 160 -
Linguine with Anchovy and Tomato Sauce - 160 -
Gnocchi with Sundried Tomatoes and Artichokes - 161 -
Pasta with Cannellini Beans - 162 -
Asian Sesame Noodles with Peanut Sauce - 163 -
Spaghetti with Olive Oil and Garlic - 164 -
Pasta Marinara - 164 -
Cheesy Meximac - 165 -
Linguine with Shrimp and Feta - 166 -
Spicy Shrimp Pasta with Olives - 167 -
Ultra Creamy Macaroni and Cheese - 168 -
Potato Gnocchi - 169 -

<u>Beef - 171 -</u>

Beef Noodle Soup - 171 -
Beef Barley Soup with Mushrooms - 172 -
BBQ Shepherd's Pie - 172 -
Swedish Meatballs - 173 -
Meatball Alphabet Soup - 173 -
Nanny's Meatballs - 174 -

Chili Con Carne - 203 -
Beef Stroganoff - 203 -
Vegetable Beef Soup with Pasta - 204 -
Shepherd's Pie - 205 -
Franks and Beans - 205 -
Kid Favorite Cheesy Mac and Beef - 206 -
Indian Beef and Corn Stew - 206 -
Easy Beefy Soup - 207 -
Crock Pot Alphabet Soup - 207 -
Slow Cooked Beef Lentil Soup - 208 -
Meatball Hoagies - 208 -
Carne Asada Tacos - 209 -

<u>Chicken and Turkey - 210 -</u>

Chicken Pasta with Cheese and Caramelized Onions - 211 -
Chicken Divan - 212 -
Chicken and Wild Rice Soup - 213 -
Chicken with Olives, Lemon and Capers - 213 -
Chicken and Dumplings - 214 -
Spiced Turkey with Rice Pilaf and Lima Beans - 215 -
Slow Cooked Green Turkey Chili - 216 -
Lemon Chicken Soup - 217 -
Chicken and Potato Pizzaiola - 217 -
Slow Cooked Chicken and Bean Stew - 218 -
Chicken Casserole - 219 -
Chicken and Rice - 220 -
Chicken Broccoli Casserole - 221 -
Chicken Noodle Mushroom Casserole - 222 -
White Chili - 223 -
Chicken Chili - 223 -
Teriyaki Turkey Breast with Pineapple - 224 -
Turkey (or Chicken) and Dumplings - 225 -
Lemon, Dijon, Rosemary Rubbed Chicken - 226 -
Chili Rubbed Chicken - 226 -

Made in the USA
San Bernardino, CA
08 March 2013